HOOK UP!

U.S. PARATROOPERS
From the Vietnam War to the Cold War

Acknowledgements

With gratitude to:

Enrique Parra for his generosity and permanent availability.

Julio Rodríguez and Miguel Ángel Blanco for their help and patience in making this project possible.

Abraham Nieto and José Luis Desimon for their selfless effort and dedication.

Miguel González and David de la Morena, Joaquín Lanza, Javier Novella, Fernando Deignacio and my colleagues at the Military Parachute School "Mendez Parada" Bernardo Expresati and Miguel Aiyón.

ISBN: 978-84-96658-55-4

DL: M-17786-2015

Published by

ANDREA PRESS
C/Talleres, 21 - Pol. Ind. de Alpedrete
28430 Alpedrete (Madrid) SPAIN
Tel.: (34) 91 857 00 08 - Fax: (34) 91 857 00 48
www.andreapresspublishing.com
sales@andreapresspublishing.com

The author is responsible for the complete contents of this book including all illustrations, photographs and text. The publisher shall not be held responsible for any copyright infringement.

Distributed in the EU by:

ANDREA EUROPE S.L.

C/Talleres, 21 - Pol. Ind. de Alpedrete
28430 Alpedrete (Madrid) SPAIN
Tel.: (34) 91 857 00 08
Fax: (34) 91 857 00 48
orders@andreaeurope.com
www.andreaeurope.com

Distributed in USA and Canada by:

ANDREA DEPOT USA, INC

1822 Holly Rd., Suite 110
Corpus Christi TX 78417 TEXAS - USA
Phone: 361-334-1625
Fax: 361-334-2955
orders@andreadepotusa.com
www.andreadepotusa.com

Authors: Alejandro Rodríguez and Antonio Arques

Editor-in-Chief: Raúl Rubio

Translator: Jane Wintle Taylor

Book Design: Andrea Press

All photos belong to private collections except:
Pages: 15, 85, 107 (Corbis)
Pages: 6, 16, 34, 39, 158 (NARA Archives)

On the front cover:
US Paratroopers of the 82nd Airborne Division based at Fort Bragg.
© JP Laffont/Sygma/Corbis.

Printed in China

INTRODUCTION

The idea of "sky fighters" dropping from the air could probably be traced back to mythological times, although the first "serious" proposals for the creation of airborne forces date from late 18th century and the first - really effective - forces of this kind debuted in WWII, achieving remarkable and well-known feats of arms.

Despite the relatively minor strategic importance often attributed to these forces, the captivating allure of these daring soldiers, their gear and the associated technical complexities have always drawn the curiosity and admiration of those interested in military history.

For these reasons, the idea for a book on paratroopers with a special focus on their equipment, training and procedures had been considered for a while at Andrea Press when Mr. Alejandro Rodríguez - very enthusiastically - contacted us for publishing this book.

Mr. Rodríguez had been gathering documentation on the history of his U.S. colleagues for a number of years while putting together at the same time the extraordinary collection of uniforms, weapons and equipment covered in this book. In addition, the fact that he had been a paratrooper NCO himself, with ample experience on the field, left few doubts - if any - for producing this book that has taken more than a year of coordinated effort by the author and Andrea Press.

Last but not least is Antonio Arques´ outstanding contribution, complementing and enhancing both the writing and pictures of this work.

Andrea Press

Glossary

AAD. Air Assault Division.

ABN BDE. Airborne Brigade.

ABN DIV. Airborne Division.

Accordion folding. Folding a canopy into folds of uniform length, accordion fashion.

ACR. Armored Cavalry Regiment.

Adapter. A rectangular metal fitting with a fixed crossbar.

Adapter, quick-fit. A rectangular metal fitting with a floating friction-grip bar.

AEB. Airborne Engineer Battalion.

Alice. All-Purpose Lightweight Individual Carrying Equipment.

Apex. The center and topmost point of an inflated canopy.

Backstrap. A part of the parachute harness that extends across the small of the back both horizontally and diagonally.

Bag, deployment. A fabric container containing a parachute canopy, often inclosed in a parachute pack. The T-10 parachute has a provision for storing the suspension lines in the bag.

Band, lower lateral. A webbing band inserted in the skirt of a canopy.

BAR. Browning Automatic Rifle.

Barnd, upper lateral. A webbing band inserted in the vent hem of a canopy.

Band, pocket. A webbing attached at the outside of the skirt, across radial seams, in a manner that causes the gores to be pulled outward at inflation, thereby improving the opening characteristics.

Band, retainer. A rubber band used to hold folded suspension lines or the static line to the parachute pack.

BDU. Battle Dress Uniform.

Breakcord. A thread or fabric tape tied between parachute components that is intended to break under desired load during deployment.

Breathing, canopy. The pulsating or pumping action of an inflated canopy during descent.

Bridle. The arrangement of cords attaching the pilot chute to the apex of the canopy or to the deployment bag.

Bungee cord. An elastic cord designed to absorb shock when a falling object (weapons case) is arrested.

Cable, ripcord. A flexible cable joining lockpins and ripcord grip.

Canopy. That portion of a parachute consisting of the drag producing surface (fabric area) and the suspension lines extended to a mutual point of confluence.

CIDG. Civilian Irregular Defense Group Program.

Cone, pack (locking cone). A small, cone-shaped metal post sewed to one of the side flaps of a parachute pack. A hole is drilled longitudinally to receive the ripcord locking pin which is attached to the ripcord cable.

COSVN. Central Office For South Vietnam.

CTZ. Corps Tactical Zone.

DA. Department Of The Army.

DA Pam. Department Of The Army Pamphlets.

Deployment. That portion of a parachute's operations occurring from the initiation of activation to the instant the suspension lines are extended but prior to inflation of the canopy.

DI. Distinctive Insignia.

Diameter, nominal. The computed diameter designation of a parachute canopy which equals the diameter of a circle having the same total area as the total cloth surface.

Diameter, projected. The outside diameter of an inflated canopy measured in the plane of the maximum cross section.

DMS. Direct Molded Sole.

DoD. Department Of Defense.

Drift. The horizontal displacement of a descending parachute.

D-ring. A metal fitting shaped like a "D" found on the T-10 parachute harness.

Drogue. A stabilizing or retarding device; e.g., a pilot parachute attached to a heavy drop load to stabilize the load after extraction and prior to deployment.

DUI. Distinctive Unit Insignia.

DZ. Drop Zone.

ERDL. Engineer Research And Development Laboratories.

Eye. A small, steel wire loop attached to a parachute pack into which is fastened the hook of a pack opening spring band.

Fasteners, parachute pack. A metal fitting secured to each end flap of a pack. The fasteners fit over locking cones and secure end flaps in a closed position until the locking pins are pulled free.

FM. Field Manual.

FSB. Fire Support Base.

GFAB. Glider Field Artillery Battalions.

GIR. Glider Infantry Regiment.

HAHO. High Altitude, High Opening.

HALO. High Altitude, Low Opening.

HBT. Herringbone Twill.

HHC. Headquarters And Headquarters Company.

ID. Infantry Division.

ILCE. Individual Load Carrying Equipment.

ILLCE. Individual Lightweight Load-Carrying Equipment.

Keepers. Length of webbing sewed on a pack or around suspension lines and adjusted to hold the pack firmly to the harness or load on which it is used, or to form a confluence point for suspension lines to prevent relative movement of lines.

LCE. Load Carrying Equipment.

Leg strap. That portion of the harness sewed to the saddle that passes under the legs from the saddle and is fastened to the leg strap loop or passes through the leg strap loop and is secured to the quick-release assembly.

LIB. Light Infantry Brigade.

Lift web. That portion of the harness comprising the main webbing support extending from the canopy release assemblies down through the saddle and up to the opposite canopy release.

Line, static. A line, cable, or webbing, one end of which is fastened to the pack, canopy, or deployment bag, and the other to some part of the launching vehicle. It is used to open a pack or deploy a canopy.

Line, suspension. Cords or webbing of silk, nylon, cotton, rayon, or other fabric, that connects the drag-producing surface (canopy) to the harness or risers.

Link, connector. A rectangular metal fitting used to connect suspension lines to risers or lift webs. Connector links may be separable.

Loop, retaining. A loop of webbing or tape, usually elastic, used to hold folded lines or excess webbing in position.

LTD. Lift The Dot.

LZ. Landing Zones.

MAAG-Vietnam. Military Assistance And Advisory Group-Vietnam.

MACV. Military Assistance Command Vietnam.

Malfunction. The complete or partial failure of a canopy to achieve proper opening within the correct time.

MLCE. Modernized Load Carrying Equipment.

NATO. North Atlantic Treaty Organization.

NCO. Non-Commissioned Officer.

NVA. North Vietnamese Army.

Pack assembly. A container that incloses the canopy and provides for a means of opening to allow deployment of the canopy. The canopy may be placed in a deployment bag or sleeve.

Pack cover. A piece of canvas or duck with a static line attached, used to cover the packed canopy.

Pack flap. A fabric extension on a side or end of the pack body designed to inclose and protect the canopy.

Pack opening spring bands. Elastic cords with a steel spring and metal hooks attached at the ends installed on a parachute pack under tension, used to separate the end flaps from the side flaps when the ripcord is pulled.

Pam. Pamphlets.

Parachute assembly. An assembly consisting of canopy, risers, or bridles, deployment bag, and in some cases, a pilot chute. The pack harness and reserve parachute are all part of the assembly.

Parachute, free type. A parachute not attached to the aircraft that is activated by the jumper.

Parachute, reserve. A second parachute worn on the chest and used in the event of a malfunction of the main parachute.

Parachute, static line type. A parachute that is activated by a static line attached to an anchor line cable or ring inside the aircraft.

PASGT. Personal Armor System For Ground Troops.

PFAB. Parachute Field Artillery Battalion.

PFC. Private First Class.

PG. Pocket Guides.

Pilot chute. A small parachute attached to the apex of a larger canopy to accelerate deployment.

Pin, locking. Short, metal prongs attached to a ripcord cable. These pins are inserted into locking cones which secure the pack flaps as a function of closing a parachute park.

PIR. Parachute Infantry Regiment.

PVDC. Polyvinylidene Chloride.

Quick-fit V-Ring. A metal fitting in form of a closed letter "V" into which quick-ejector snaps are hooked and it has a floating friction grip crossbar to facilitate securing of webbing.

RCT. Regimental Combat Team.

RDF. Rapid Deployment Force.

Release, canopy. A device designed to permit rapid separation of the canopy from the harness.

Release, harness. A device designed to permit rapid separation of the harness from the wearer. Referred to as the quick release assembly in this manual.

Ripcord. A device that consists of a cable, locking pins, and a grip which activates the parachute when pulled or released.

Riser. A high strength material attached to the harness which secures the suspension lines by means of connector links.

ROTC. Army Reserve Officers' Training Corps.

RON. Remain Overnight Positions.

RTO. Radio/Telephone Operator.

Saddle. That portion of the harness that is positioned in the main lift web at the seat of the wearer.

Sail. A term used to designate a condition noted in the deployment of a parachute canopy when the canopy is still attached to the static line and is exposed broadside to the airstream. With the T-10 parachute this condition exists with the canopy still in the deployment bag.

SF. Special Forces.

Skirt. The reinforced hem forming the periphery of the canopy.

Sleeve. A tapered, fabric tube in which a canopy is placed to control its deployment.

Slipping. A method of controlling an inflated canopy in a desired direction by spilling the air from one side of the skirt by manipulation of the risers. This action causes an increased average rate of descent until the lines are released.

Slot. A vent constructed in a gore of a canopy.

Snap, connector. A hook-shaped, spring-loaded metal fitting.

Snaphook, static line. A metal device used to connect the free end of the static line to a cable or ring in an aircraft.

Squidding. A state of incomplete canopy inflation in which the canopy is pear-shaped. Excessive airspeed is the cause.

Stow. Any one loop of static line or suspension line compactly secured to the parachute pack.

Strength, tensile. The tension, measured in pounds, required to break a material when pulled or stretched.

SSI. Shoulder Sleeve Insignias.

TC. Training Circulars.

TM. Technical Manual.

USAF. Us Air Force.

USARV. Us Army Vietnam.

VC. Vietcong.

Vent. Any opening in the cloth surface of the canopy, as an apex vent.

Table of Contents

Acknowledgments 2

Introduction   3

Glossary   4

Index   7

1. US Paratroopers in History 11

2. Operation "Junction City" 15

3. From Boot Camp to combat 19
   3.1. Basic Airborne Course 19
   3.2. Five Points of Performance 20
   3.3. Jump procedure 21
         3.3.1. Jump commands 22

4. Getting equipped step by step 25
   4.1. Donning the T-10 Parachute Assembly: the "Buddy System" 25

5. Gear   35
   5.1. Headgear 35
         5.1.1. M1C Parachutist's Helmet 35
         5.1.2. M1C Parachutist's Helmet Shell 36
         5.1.3. M1C Parachutist's Helmet Liner 37
   5.2. Uniforms 40
         5.2.1. Utility Uniform 41
         5.2.2. Tropical Uniform 45
         5.2.3. ERDL Tropical Uniform 47
   5.3. Footgear 49
         5.3.1. Paratrooper Leather Boots 49
         5.3.2. Tropical Boots 50
               1st Model 50
               2nd Model 52
               3rd Model 52
               4th Model 53
   5.4. Individual Combat Equipment 54
         5.4.1. Pistol Belt 56
         5.4.2. Suspenders 58
         5.4.3. Field Pack 59
         5.4.4. Ammunition Pouch 62
         5.4.5. First Aid/Compass Pouch 64
         5.4.6. Entrenching Tool and Carrier 65

C Fred L. Greenleaf crosses a deep irrigation canal along with other members of the mpany who are enroute to a Viet Cong controlled village. (NARA archives).

5.4.7. Canteen and Cover 1 qt.. 66

5.4.8. Canteen and Cover 2 qt.. 68

5.4.9. Sleeping Bag Carrying Strap Assembly 71

6. Parachutists´ equipment.. 73

6.1. Parachute components.. 73

6.1.1. Canopy assembly.. 73

6.1.1.1. MC1 Canopy assembly... 73

6.1.1.2. MC1 Maneuverable Canopy assembly... 75

6.1.1.3. MC1 Maneuverable Modified Canopy assembly.. 76

6.1.1.4. MC1-1 Canopy assembly.. 76

6.1.2. Deployment Bag 77

6.1.3. Pack Tray or Parachute Pack... 81

6.1.3.1. Pack tray of cotton material with waistband located at center of pack tray... 81

6.1.3.2. Pack tray of nylon material with waistband located at center of pack tray ... 83

6.1.3.3. Pack tray of nylon material with waistband attached in a lower position 83

6.1.4. Parachute risers 84

6.1.4.1. T-10 Parachute risers... 84

6.1.4.2. T-10 Maneuverable Parachute Risers.. 85

6.1.4.3. T-10 Maneuverable Parachute Modified Risers.. 86

6.1.4.4. MC1-1 Parachute Risers.. 87

6.1.5. Harness Assembly 89

6.1.5.1. Harness Assembly with Harness Quick-Release Assemblies................................ 89

6.1.5.1.1 Canopy release assembly with pressure type release............................ 90

6.1.5.2. Harness Assembly with 3 Quick-Ejector Snaps... 91

6.1.5.2.1. Canopy release assembly with cable loop type release....................... 93

6.1.6. Harness Quick-Release Assembly 94

6.2. Parachute models 96

6.2.1. T-10 Main Troop-Back Parachute.. 96

6.2.1.1. 35-foot diameter T-10 troop back parachute assembly.................................... 96

6.2.1.2. 35-foot diameter T-10 maneuverable troop back parachute assembly 97

6.2.1.3. 35-foot diameter T-10 maneuverable modified troop back parachute assembly .. 99

6.2.1.4. 35-foot diameter T-10A troop back parachute assembly.................................. 100

6.2.1.5. 35-foot diameter T-10B troop back parachute assembly. 100

6.2.2. MC1-1 main troop-back parachute.. 101

6.2.2.1. 35-foot diameter MC1-1 troop back parachute assembly................................ 101

6.2.2.2. 35-foot diameter MC1-1A troop back parachute assembly.............................. 101

6.2.2.3. 35-foot diameter MC1-1B troop back parachute assembly 101

6.2.3. T-10 Reserve Parachute 102

6.2.3.1. Pilot chute. 104

6.2.3.2. Canopy assembly. 104

6.2.3.3. Pack assembly. 105

6.2.3.4. Ripcord 105

6.3. Combat Loads 106

6.3.1. Wearing of Combat Equipment... 108

6.3.1.1. Wearing of unit Combat Equipment... 108

6.3.1.2. Wearing of Individual Combat Equipment.. 108

6.3.1.2.1. Steel Helmet... 108

6.3.1.2.2. Individual Equipment Belt "Pistol Belt"... 108

6.3.1.2.3. Combat Field Pack Suspenders 109

6.3.1.2.4. Universal Small Arms Ammunition Pouch 109

6.3.1.2.5. Combat Field Pack "Butt Pack"... 110

6.3.1.2.6. First Aid/Compass Pouch.. 110

6.3.1.2.7. Canteen with Cup and Cover 110

6.3.1.2.8. Entrenching Tool with Carrier and Bayonet with Scabbard............ 111
6.3.1.2.9. MC-1 Parachutist´s Knife.. 111
6.3.1.2.10. Ammunition and Hand Grenades.. 111
6.3.1.2.12. M17 Protective Field Mask... 111
6.3.2. Individual equipment 112
6.3.2.1. Weapons 112
6.3.2.1.1. M14 Rifle... 112
6.3.2.1.2. M16 and M16A1 Rifle... 114
6.3.2.1.3. M79 Grenade Launcher.. 116
6.3.2.1.4. M60 Machine Gun.. 117
6.3.2.1.5. Pistol... 117
6.3.2.1.6. Other weapons.. 117
6.3.2.2. H Harness.. 118
6.3.2.2.1. Aviator's Kit Bag 118
6.3.2.2.2. Rucksack 121
6.3.3. Personnel Equipment Containers 124
6.3.3.1. Adjustable Individual Weapons Case M1950 124
6.3.3.2. Adjustable Equipment Bag 126
6.3.3.3. Weapons and Individual Equipment Container and Harness Assembly...... 130
6.3.3.3.1. Weapon and Individual Equipment Harness Assembly 131
6.3.3.3.2. Weapon and Individual Equipment Container........................... 133

7. Insignias 137

7.1. Shoulder Sleeve Insignias 137
7.2. Regimental Distinctive Unit Insignias... 140
7.3. Skills Badges and other parachutist's insignias 141
7.3.1. Parachutist's Badge 141
7.3.2. Rigger Badge 144
7.3.3. Pathfinder Badge... 144
7.3.4. Ranger and Recon Badges 145
7.3.5. Parachutists´ Badge Ovals 145
7.3.6. Paraglider Patch and Beret Flashes 148

8. Manual, Pamphlets and Paper Miscellanea................................153

8.1. Field and Technical Manuals 154
8.2. Parachutists Manuals 154
8.3. Parachutists´ paper miscellanea 156

Bibliography 159

Corporal Louis E. Laird, of the 101st Airborne Division, fully equipped, boards a C-47 transport aircraft for an exercise in the spring of 1944. The complete division, together with the 82nd Airborne Division, was dropped over France on the eve of the Allied landing on Normandy on 6 June 1944.

1. US Paratroopers in History

Military parachuting in the US Army began as a consequence of experiments in this field after WWI and observing the successful outcomes in other countries such as the Soviet Union and Germany in the 1930s. The use made by the Germans of their parachute troops in the Blitzkrieg, spearheading assaults on the Netherlands and northern Europe in April and May 1940, was particularly important for the effect it had on the development of parachute techniques in the United States and Great Britain.

In April 1940, after a year spent studying how to define parachuting in the US Army, authorization was given for a test unit to be formed, the Test Platoon of Airborne Infantry. This order had materialized by

the middle of the year at Fort Benning, in the form of a platoon with a lieutenant, six non-commissioned officers and forty two privates detached from the 29th Infantry Regiment. This test platoon, under the control of the Infantry Board, performed an eight-week course comprising rigorous physical training, learning landing techniques and jump practice from a 125-foot tower. By mid-August, each m an had made several jumps from an aircraft and, in the final week, on 29 August, a mass jump was conducted.

In September, after the success of the test platoon, the 1st Parachute Battalion was founded, the first parachute combat unit in the US Army (later renamed 501st Parachute Battalion).

In 1941 this battalion gained further experience and continued to train paratroopers. By year's end the Department of War decided to create three further parachute Battalions, the 502nd, 503rd and 504th Parachute Battalions. Since the test platoon, these units were made up of volunteers, some of whom, owing to the small number of places, renounced their non-commissioned officer ranks in order to become paratroopers.

Having passed the basic jump course, they received their silver paratrooper's wings and went on to a 16-week period of exercises at squad, platoon, company and battalion level. As well as receiving their paratrooper rating, the men underwent physical training, long

General Eisenhower, Commander of Allied troops in Europe, speaks to the paratroopers of the 101st Airborne Division moments before their deployment over France on D-Day.

11

marches and runs, scouting, patrolling, orientation using compass and map, and familiarization with every kind of weapon liable to be airborne.

In early 1942 the order was given to form four paratrooper regiments from the four existing battalions. Throughout that year, the newly formed regiments had to recruit and train their soldiers to qualify them as paratroopers. At the same time, the first airborne divisions (were created Abn Div) in the US Army, the 82nd and 101st, which to begin with were smaller than an infantry division. As further new paratrooper regiments were established, in 1943 three further divisions were created, the 11th, the 13th and the 17th Abn Div. Following the first combat experience in WWII, the airborne divisions were strengthened, reaching 16.800 men and 870 vehicles, organized in three Parachute Infantry Regiments (PIR), two Glider Infantry Regiments (GIR), one Parachute Field Artillery

Battalion (PFAB), two Glider Field Artillery Battalions (GFAB), one Airborne Engineer Battalion (AEB) and several ancillary units.

The first to act in WWII was the 503rd PIR which was launched in November 1942 over north Africa in Operation Torch. In 1943, the 82nd Abn Div was sent into combat in that region, and continued with the invasion of Sicily, where airborne troops were dropped on Syracuse and, later, in Salerno during the subsequent campaign in Italy.

The 101st Abn Div set out for Great Britain in 1943, and was joined in 1944 by the 82nd Abn Div, in preparation for the airborne assault on Normandy. Later, both divisions took part in other airborne operations and in further fighting on the ground up to the end of the war. The 17th and 13th divisions were also sent to Europe, the former being parachuted in while the latter relieved other battle weary divisions. The 11th Abn Div was sent to the

Pacific theatre of operations, where it made several combat jumps.

After WWII some paratrooper divisions and regiments were deactivated. The only ones to remain active were the 11th Abn Div, stationed in Japan, and the 82nd Abn Div at Fort Bragg, in the role of rapid reaction strategic forces. When war broke out in Korea, only the 187th PIR, separated form the 11th Abn Div and reconfigured as a Regimental Combat Team, was sent to that theatre where it made several combat jumps. In 1957 the 101st Abn Div was reactivated, while the 11th Abn Div was sent to Germany and, later, deactivated. Also in Germany, a portion of this division became part of the 24th Infantry Division (ID), which in this way gained partial airborne capability.

In 1958, airborne troops of the 24th ID were sent to Lebanon as part of the Task Force to re-establish order in the region. Shortly afterward, the airborne function of the 24th ID in Germany was transferred to the 8th ID and, in addition, a new airborne unit was activated in the Pacific, the 173rd Airborne Brigade (Abn Bde), based on the 503rd PIR that was relieved from the 82nd Airborne Brigade.

In February 1963 the 11th Division was reactivated, now as the 11th Air Assault Division (Test) to serve as test unit in the trials for the creation of a heliborne division. Once the tests had been successfully completed, in 1965, the division was absorbed by the new 1st Cavalry Division (Airmobile), that would immediately receive orders to deploy to Vietnam. The 173rd Abn Bde was one of the first units to be called in by General Westmoreland, Commander of Military Assistance Command Vietnam (MACV), and arrived in the country in early May 1965. This brigade fought in Vietnam until August 1971, shortly after which it was deactivated. One of its battalions, the 2/503, performed the only combat jump made by American paratroopers in the entire Vietnam War.

Paratroopers get ready for a training jump from an aircraft, in August 1943.

The 101st Abn Div sent a brigade to Vietnam in July 1965, and the rest of the division arrived toward the end of 1967. The lack of personnel qualified as paratroopers and the success of the airmobility concept with the massive use of helicopters, led the division to be reconfigured as the 101st Airborne Division (Airmobile) in mid-1969. The division remained in Vietnam until early 1972, serving thereafter in the US Army as an airmobile division though it retained its airborne title for the sake of tradition.

The 82nd Abn Div, as a strategic rapid reaction unit, was called in to act in the Dominican Republic where civil war threatened the interests and the lives of US citizens in the country. In combat with the rebels, the division suffered 60 casualties, and the first brigade stayed in the theatre until September 1966. In Vietnam, General Westmoreland requested the 82nd to reinforce the military capacity of the MACV, particularly after the communist Tet offensive in February 1968. However, as it formed part of the strategic reserve, only one brigade was authorized, the third, which landed in Vietnam that very month. With Nixon's arrival in the White House and the setting in motion of the "vietnamisation" of the conflict, this brigade was one of the first to be repatriated, and it was sent home in December 1969.

In Vietnam, with the exception of the combat jump by the 173rd Abn Bde, paratroopers acted as infantry and made massive use of the helicopter as air assault vehicle. After the war, thanks to the successful role played by helicopters, the need to maintain parachute units was questioned. These voices were silenced partly owing to the units' long distance deployment capability. In 1983, during the invasion of the island of Grenada, the 82nd Abn Div was air-transported to the area while two battalions of the 75th Infantry Regiment (Ranger) were dropped over their objectives. The usefulness of paratrooper units in the US Armed Forces remained after the Cold War and is still current today.

After the Lessons Learned during WW2, military parachuting continued to improve its aircraft and equipment.

General William C. Lee was born in 1895 and graduated as an officer of the US Army from the ROCT program at North Carolina State University. After WWI he was sent to Germany as observer, and in 1930, after attending Tank School, he was sent to France for advanced training. Then, as expert in the new armor combat theory, he became an instructor at the Infantry School at Fort Benning.

In 1939 he was posted to Washington as expert in armored combat at the Office of the Chief of Infantry. There, impressed by the development of the German parachute troops and their innovative tactics, he studied paratroopers' actions during the beginning of WWII and advocated their inclusion in the US Army, against the opinions of high ranking chiefs in the Armed Forces. Backed by president Franklin Roosevelt, he was commissioned to assess the feasibility of a parachute unit and was assigned to lead the project.

In 1940 he organized the test parachute platoon and subsequently became the first commander of the Airborne School in Fort Benning, Georgia. He commanded the United States Airborne Command, set up in March 1942, and from August that year became the first Commander of the 101st Airborne Division.

Lee attached special importance to his troops' training, and established a rigorous program that included the basic parachute course at the jumpschool, followed by orientation exercises, physical training and field maneuvers. For his achievements, Lee was awarded the Distinguished Service Medal and promoted to the rank of Major General.

In Great Britain he trained his division for the assault on Normandy on D-Day, and with his assistant General Pratt, drew up plans for the airborne phase called Operation Overlord. In February 1944 he suffered a heart attack and was relieved as commander of the 101st Abn Div by General Taylor.

Lee is recognized as instrumental to the success of the invasion of Normandy and as the Father of the American Paratrooper.

RTOs transmit information on the 173rd Airborne Brigade's operations. Until it was replaced with the PRC-25, the brigade used the PRC-10 as field radio. This unit was one of the first to use the new M-16 assault rifle in Vietnam.

2. Operation "Junction City"

In November 1966, Military Assistance Command Vietnam (MACV) ordered LtGen Seaman, commander of the II Field Force, to "think big" in terms of an offensive in the III Corps Tactical Zone (CTZ) in 1967. An ambitious idea was formed to send American and South Vietnamese troops to War Zone C, dominated by the Vietcong (VC), north of Saigon and close to the border with Cambodia. The operation, named Junction City, was the largest to be launched by the United States since the beginning of the war, in a push to reach the enemy's neuralgic center making massive use of tanks and airborne troops.

MACV intelligence reports drew a worrying picture of the VC forces in the Iron Triangle, an area between Saigon and War Zone C. Seaman received warning that he would first have to clear the area, and in mid-December the assault on War Zone C was postponed while a preliminary operation named Cedar Falls launched an attack on the Iron Triangle.

Cedar Falls was designed as a 'hammer and anvil' operation to clear an area of thick jungle and humid rice paddies, of which the southernmost point was just 20 km from the outskirts of Saigon. A brigade of the 25th Infantry Division (ID), augmented by the 196th Light Infantry Brigade (LIB), had to secure and search the western arm of the Triangle, while two brigades of the 1st Infantry Division, the 11th Armored Cavalry Regiment (ACR) and the 173rd Airborne Brigade (Abn Bde) took care of the eastern side.

With the 25th ID remaining in place as the anvil, the others acted as hammers sweeping to the west and the south. The objective was to drive communist support of any kind out of the Iron Triangle. This involved taking villages, deporting the population by force, and destroying everything of value from jungle canopy and crops to houses, tunnel complexes and military installations. It was also intended that the headquarters of the IV Military Region of the VC, responsible for coordinating operations around Saigon, would be destroyed.

The operation took place from 8 to 26 January, with a confirmed death toll of 759 VC against 72 Americans dead and 337 wounded. Nevertheless, the 9th VC Division avoided being captured during the operation and escaped the horseshoe, although it left behind several underground complexes discovered by American troops. The preliminary operation was ended when the troops involved were needed for Operation Junction City. The absence of any long-term impact was made clear by the fact that the VC recommenced their activities in the Triangle less than 48 hours later.

War Zone C was a relatively flat area of about 2200 km^2, limiting to the north and the west with Cambodia, to the east with Route 13, and to the south with a line drawn from Tay Ninh City to Ben Cat. It offered fairly good conditions for armored or mechanized units, with sufficient clear spaces to build Fire Support Bases (FSB) and landing zones (LZ). This region had been under communist domination for at least 20 years, and the aim of Operation Junction City was to wipe out

Paratroops deploy over War Zone C during Operation Junction City, a drive against the Vietcong held villages on the Cambodian border during the Vietnam War.

that control and convince the communists that none of their primary strongholds inside South Vietnam were safe any more.

In the process, it was expected that the Central Office for South Vietnam (COSVN), the main communist headquarters, responsible for the coordination of all operations throughout the south, would be identified and destroyed. As MACV intelligence reports showed that the enemy forces in the Iron Triangle –belonging to the 9th VC Division and the 101st North Vietnamese Army (NVA) Regiment– were in the western part of the area, Seaman sent his units there.

Preliminary deception operations were to place American units at the western and eastern edges of the area. Operation Gadsden, from 2 to 20 February, planted the 25th ID in Lo Go, on the western edge, while Operation Tucson, from 14 to 17 February, deployed two brigades from the 1st ID to the east in the Binh Long area. During Phase One of Junction City, planned for 22 January 1967, these troops moved northward, close to the border with Cambodia, to form a horseshoe blocking the west, north and east. Another brigade, with armored support, would then attack the horseshoe open at the south to trap the NVA/VC and perform searches. To ensure that the area remained open for future US operations, the Special Forces (SF) and the indigenous CIDG militia would build camps to the north of Tay Ninh City, with an airstrip able to handle C-130 aircraft carrying supplies or reinforcements.

Phase One of Junction City started in an unaccustomed manner, with nine infantry battalions (from the 1st ID and the 173rd Abn Bde) airlifted to a number of preselected LZ along the northern rim of the horseshoe, reinforced the next day with the 2nd brigade, 25th ID and the 11th ACR from the south. A total of 249 helicopters lifted eight of these battalions to their positions, while the ninth assault was performed by means of the only combat parachute jump in the Vietnam War.

Dropping the 173rd Abn Bde required making helicopters available for the remainder of the operation. It was also claimed that the whole battalion could be deployed in a shorter time. Early on 22 February, all 845 men (mostly from the 2nd Battalion, 503rd Parachutist Infantry Regiment led by LtCol Sigholtz) were transferred by truck to Bien Hoa, where 16 C-130 aircraft awaited them. Their heavy packs were set out on the tarmac, each weighing some 100 or 115 pounds, including the T-10 parachute and combat equipment, around 22 M-16 ammo clips, several canteens of water, and rations, as well as collective equipment such as 200 cartridges for the squad machine gun and the PRC-10 radios. At 08:25 h the planes took

off and half an hour later opened their doors letting the damp warm Vietnam air fill the cargo bays. The jumpmasters initiated the jump procedure. The men stood up and shuffled toward the doors, with their heavy packs and weapons strapped to their legs. At 09:00 the drop commenced over the selected area, marked with colored smoke delivered by forward air controller teams. At 09:20 command posts had been set up on the ground and five minutes later, the heavy equipment started to arrive. After the jump, the battalion set off through the tall, razor-sharp elephant grass that considerably reduced visibility. Then each company had to cut a path through the bamboo using machetes, at which the men leading the column took turns. Radio contact was maintained to coordinate movements, and at nightfall they would stop to set up RONs (Remain Overnight Position), digging foxholes in the hard ground and placing sandbags, reinforcing the perimeter with booby traps and trip flares. By the end of the day, the brigade had just 11 minor injuries, all from the jump, and no contact had been made with the enemy.

To all purposes, Phase One of Junction City was a success, and the Americans established a strong presence in an area that had been a communist haven. Some major discoveries were made, such as when on 28 February the 173rd Abn Bde found the Vietcong Central Informa-

tion Office, with a photography lab, propaganda pamphlets and other documents. American troops also fought a number of important battles, in particular against the 101st NVA and 272nd VC regiments, in which they prevailed thanks to the effective use of artillery support and tactical bombing.

Phase Two of Junction City began on 18 March, with the deployment of the 1st ID supported by the 11th ACR. The 173th Abn Bde was replaced by a brigade from the 9th ID. The infantry conducted search and destroy missions, while mechanized units kept the An Loc route open to ensure that supplies reached the engineers building the new bases and airstrips for the SF. The daily 200-truck convoys traveled on Route 13 from Saigon to An Loc, and then turned west escorted by armored vehicles of the 11th ACR and protected by the guns at the newly built FSB along the route. In view of the successful outcome of Phase Two, on 15 April the US Command added a third phase, that would last until 14 May, with a brigade from the 25th ID performing search missions.

All in all, the operation was a complex plan in which more than 25,000 US and South Vietnamese soldiers took part, and contact with the enemy was limited to five mas-

sive assaults by the Vietcong, all of which were repulsed. Casualties totaled 2,728 dead, 34 prisoners and 139 desertions on the Vietcong side, with the Americans counting 282 dead and 1576 wounded.

For the US command, Junction City was a turning point, after penetrating and causing severe damage to the communist sanctuary in War Zone C, and the operational concept of a large-scale multi-organization was declared a success, although it was difficult to measure

the overall impact of the operation. The COSVN had not been destroyed: in fact, it merely retreated to Cambodia; and as the American units were needed elsewhere, not enough forces remained in War Zone C or the Iron Triangle to prevent a rapid communist recovery. Once again, firepower and mobility had been used to mount operations within communist territory and cause damage, but the temporary nature of these incursions meant that the enemy could always reclaim its safe havens in the jungle.

Operation Junction City involved a large number of troops, and part of their supplies were air dropped by the USAF Military Airlift Command. In this photograph an M88 recovery vehicle can be seen on the right.

Members of the 4th Battalion, 503rd Infantry, 173rd Airborne Brigade being heli-lifted by UH-1D Helicopters, in a preliminary operation to Junction City in September 1966. (Photo NARA archives).

3. From Boot Camp to combat

Military parachuting was a voluntary service in the US Armed Forces. Before enrolling for the airborne course, aspiring paratroopers first had to complete the basic Boot Camp training, mandatory for all US Army recruits. This was the 8-week Basic Combat Training Course during which core skills were learned and students graduated as soldiers. The course was followed by further professional development in military occupational specialties; in this case, Infantryman (11-B). For eight weeks in the Infantry Advanced Individual Training Course, soldiers received instruction in combat techniques and handling of equipment, and spent an additional week of special preparation for the war in Vietnam.

Paratrooper volunteers were required to pass the Airborne Physical Fitness Test, following which they went to Jump School at Fort Benning where they underwent physical endurance training and learned specific parachute techniques.

3.1. Basic Airborne Course

The US Army Jump School is at Fort Benning, Georgia, since the volunteer Test Platoon was established in 1940. This is where the Basic Airborne Course, advanced parachuting, Pathfinder and Jumpmaster courses are given.

In the 1960s and 70s, volunteers who were accepted for parachute training went to Fort Benning, Georgia, to attend the Basic Airborne Course as members of the School Brigade, consisting of nine companies (41st - 49th Student Company). Their situation during this course, as privates, was quite different to Boot Camp. They were no longer treated as novices, the meals were good, the officers treated them correctly and the NCOs had their own business to attend to and did not harass them.

On the premise that before jumping out of an airplane one has to know how to land safely, the course is divided into one week to learn to land, another week to practice handling the parachute in the air and a third week for actual jumps. Throughout all three weeks, each day began with a minimum of one hour PT and soldiers developed their physical condition meeting challenges such as four-mile runs in thirty-five minutes. Those who could not keep up this pace had to abandon the course and return to the infantry.

In the first week of training, called Ground Week, students studied and practiced the movements and positions they would need to adopt during jumps. Special attention was paid to moving inside the aircraft, jump position, parachute control during descent, landing and handling the chute on the ground.

The equipment used during this week to simulate real situations included the Mock Door to practice exits; a thirty-four foot tower to jump from in harness and attached to a riser, to feel the pull of a chute opening; and the Lateral Drift Apparatus to practice landing in a crosswind.

The second week, called Tower Week, was spent in honing the techniques learned. The Swing Training Ladder was used to practice landings. Using the Suspended Harness, students learned to remove their harness in case of emergency, such as getting strung up in a tree or falling into the sea. In the Wind Machine, students were taught to handle their chute on the ground in high wind conditions. And on the 250-foot Free Tower, the final challenge, students were raised to that height and dropped, wearing a parachute with the canopy open. The catchword was "keep your feet and knees together". After two jumps from the tower, the instructor decided whether the student was ready to go on to the third week.

During the third week, or Jump Week, students were instructed in chute failure theory and learned about different aircraft types, which in the sixties were chiefly the C-119 and the C-130. At this stage, students made real jumps from an airplane. After the first jump, each student received his wings, and went on to perform a further four jumps, one of them at night. Soldiers successfully completing the three weeks' training were considered Airborne Qualified and entitled to wear their silver jump wings with pride.

250-Foot Free Tower, part of the parachute training installations at Fort Benning, in 1968.

West Point Cadets practice exiting from an aircraft during their parachute training course at Fort Benning, Ga., in June 1962.

Harnessed to this open canopy, a student is raised to the top of the 250-Foot Free Tower.

3.2. Five Points of Performance

In view of the risks involved in parachuting, safety needed to be monitored at all times. During the Basic Airborne Training, instructors insist that students learn and practice a number of points on which their successful landings depend. These are known as the Five Points of Performance, and are drilled on the different equipment used throughout the course.

The first consists of adopting the correct position at the door of the aircraft and, on exiting, counting "One thousand, two thousand, three thousand, four thousand", which equals the time taken by the T-10 parachute to open when jumping from a plane at 115 knots. If the chute has not opened after this count, the jumper must figure out what is wrong and if necessary deploy his reserve chute.

The second point, after feeling the tug signaling an opening canopy, is to check the correct condition of the canopy and risers. If there is a twist in the risers, and the rate of descent is faster than fellow jumpers, the reserve parachute must be activated.

In a mass jump, parachutists risk colliding with other jumpers in the air. To avoid this, the third point of performance must be observed: keep a sharp lookout during the entire descent, and maneuver with the risers to avoid fellow jumpers and obstacles on the ground.

Point four is preparing to land and preventing injury when hitting the ground. This entails watching the wind conditions, holding the risers and keeping the legs straight. In the event of landing in trees, the jumper must adopt a predetermined position with his arms to protect his head. If a jumper is drifting toward a body of water, the preparatory movements include activating the quick-release to jettison the equipment rapidly once in the water and avoid sinking.

The last point is landing. This is when the majority of injuries are incurred, and techniques are learned to adapt the body position to landing sideways, forward or backward.

Ready for boarding the aircraft, 101st Airborne Division paratroopers take a break wearing their T-10 parachutes and LCE M1956 combat gear.

3.3. Jump procedure

Paratroopers put on their kit on the tarmac, by the aircraft, in pairs following a "buddy system", under the supervision of the rigger acting as jumpmaster. Aboard the plane, jumpers take to their seats and wait for orders. When the aircraft is approaching five minutes from the target, the jumpmaster and the USAF aircrewman open the side doors, or the rear ramp, depending on the type of aircraft. Two minutes from the target, the jumpmaster calls "Get ready", and then "Stand up". The men line up to form two sticks, and when the sign is given, attach the hook on their static line to the cable near the ceiling of the plane. Each jumper's static line and pack is given a visual check and the jumpmaster shouts "Stand in the door": the first man in each stick stands next to the door and adopts the jump position. At the command "Go" the drop begins and jumpers exit the aircraft in rapid succession.

Paratroopers of the 101st Airborne Division form a line to board a C-119 for a jump in full combat gear.

During the 1950s and 60s, the Fairchild C-119 Flying Boxcar was the most widely used aircraft for paratroopers, until it was replaced by the Lockheed C-130 Hercules. Both planes had the capability to drop large, heavy cargo loads from the rear hatch, and paratroopers exited from the side doors. This made drop operations faster and reduced troop dispersion on landing.

Men from the same company were dropped from different aircraft so that, should any of the aircraft be unable to perform the drop, the company would not be seriously undermanned and could continue with its assigned mission. As soon as they had landed, troops had to regroup in their respective companies, for which assembly points were established and assisted with color codes or symbols. During the drop prior to the amphibious assault on Normandy, paratroopers wore a symbol stenciled on the side of their M-1 helmets to identify their regiment and battalion, and during Operation Junction City each company wore a colored tape attached to the camouflage cover on their helmets to help troops find their unit and regroup quickly.

The troopers need to reach the ground combat-ready. On landing, they have to control the canopy and jettison their parachute.

Jump commands

To ensure positive control of the activities of jumpers inside the aircraft immediately prior to exiting, a sequence of jump commands is given by the jumpmaster. Each command requires specific actions from every jumper, and when executed properly, will insure a safe exit from the aircraft. The commands are given orally but, because of the noise from the aircraft engines they are difficult to hear. Therefore, arm-and-

1. Get ready!   **2. Outboard personnel, stand up!**

3. Inboard personnel, stand up!   **4. Hook up!**

hand signals are used with each command, given vigorously with smooth, coordinated movements. These commands, with minor varia-tions, are used in all Army and Air Force aircraft. Jumpmasters must ensure that they use the correct se-quence pertaining to each aircraft.

The commands should be explained to the jumpers in the pre-jump brief-ing. The sequence of commands used for a fully loaded C-130 air-craft is listed below:

5. Check static lines!

6. Check equipment!

7. Sound off for equipment check!

8. Stand in the door!

9. GO!

Lieutenant Colonel Robert L. Clark, Army Advisor to 2nd Special Forces Group, dons the T-10 parachute, assisted by a rigger, for a training jump in October 1961.

4. Getting equipped step by step

4.1. Donning the T-10 Parachute Assembly: the "Buddy System"

Paratroopers had to observe a rigorous procedure when donning their full pack ensuring maximum safety. The idea was that this process should serve as a further equipment check and facilitate inspection by the jumpmaster, as well as reducing discomfort for the soldier aboard the plane and when the chute is opening.

Parachute assemblies are laid on their backs with the straps extended. The quick-release assembly is left in the "locked" position.

The diagonal backstraps are loosened to the maximum.

Each man received from the rigger a parachute assembly with the contents sealed and ready for use, but attaching this to the body required manipulating a complex set of harness. The buddy system consists in forming pairs of jumpers, or buddies, who will help each other to don their packs and check all their components. At the same time, this method was useful in training new paratroopers, who were paired with more veteran jumpers. This system was used throughout the Armed Forces, under different names: "Wingmen" in the Air Force, "Battle Buddies" in the US Army, and "Shipmates" in the US Navy.

The course focused first on donning the parachute assembly and learning the names of all its components, under the instructors' permanent supervision.

The jumper's buddy lifts the parachute by the main lift web.

In the buddy system, the first step is for each jumper to inspect the exterior of the assembly, checking for visible defects, while loosening the harness to let out maximum slack. Then, jumper no. 1 receives his parachute from jumper no. 2, who holds it up and fits it on the back of jumper no. 1. The shoulder straps can now be secured, followed by the lower straps, which the buddy helps to pass under the jumper's legs. As soon as one jumper has donned his parachute it is the other jumper's turn.

When both jumpers are wearing their parachute assembly, each checks the correct adjustment of his buddy's chute. Finally, both jumpers have to don the reserve parachute, fixing it over their stomach with the backpack waistband and securing it to the parachute harness D-rings.

The jumper adopts the modified 'high jumper' position to receive the parachute assembly.

The jumper puts his arms through the opening in the shoulder straps so that the backpack rests high on his back.

The soldier adjusts the saddle around his buttocks and the assembly is secured in position.

The two chest straps are attached to the quick-release assembly, and the safety clip is inserted.

The kit bag, folded and with the carrying handle at the top, is placed against the chest and the right-hand chest strap is passed through the handle. This ensures that it is at hand to recover the parachute assembly after landing.

The jumper's buddy calls out "Right leg strap", and hands this strap under the jumper's legs.

The jumper takes the strap and confirms, calling "Right leg strap".

The leg strap is then passed through the leg strap loop, and is turned and inserted into the quick-release assembly.

101st Airborne Division paratroopers Spc. 4 George Sparrow and PFC Richard Liess, equipped for a jump exercise in June 1963. They are wearing a T-10 parachute, utility uniforms and "Corcoran" boots.

This is repeated with the left leg strap.

The jumper holds the leg strap with one hand, checking with the other for twists.

The leg strap is passed through the leg strap loop, from the inside to the outside, and turned for insertion into the quick-release assembly.

Likewise, he checks that the quick-release assembly is centered on his chest and about 12 inches below his chin.

When the harness is secured, the jumper checks that the canopy release assembly is level with his armpits.

The buddy then locates and hands to the jumper the end of the diagonal backstrap, although it is also customary for the buddy to give the harness straps an initial tightening.

The jumper pulls the diagonal backstrap close to his body.

Any excess in the backstraps must be rolled up and secured under the elastic keepers.

Both buddies, fully equipped with their parachute assembly, now face each other for a visual inspection and to fix any discrepancies.

The jumper holds the reserve parachute with his left arm, passing the waistband through the handles and the two retaining bands.

The reserve connector snaps are attached to the harness D-rings.

The buddies help each other to tighten their waistbands and secure them in quick-release form, for easy opening after landing.

Experienced paratroopers may don their parachute assembly single-handedly. The procedure in this case is similar to when using the buddy system, but each step is carried out individually. The main difference is that the jumper, holding the backpack on his knees, takes it by the straps and, in a turning movement, swings the parachute onto his back. Then he adjusts the harness in the same order as described above.

The jumper now makes a preliminary inspection of his parachute assembly.

The jumper takes the main lift webs with arms crossed to turn the parachute assembly as he hoists it onto his back.

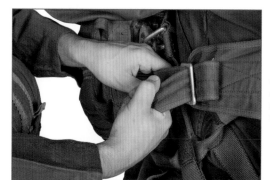

It is advisable to have a helping hand when adjusting the diagonal backstraps and securing the waistband.

Sequence of a jump exercise by members of 2nd Special Forces Group, from a C-119 "Flying Boxcar" in October 1962, over Clinton County AFB.

Despite being veteran paratroopers, the men tense waiting for the signal to jump.

The jumpmaster checks the location of the Drop Zone (DZ) at his jump bay.

The jumpmaster readies a jump "stick" (group of five troopers) for a leap into the DZ.

Paratroopers hook their static lines to the anchor cable before peeling out of the bay at the jumpmaster's signal.

"Stand in the door" is the command given by the jumpmaster as he signals a trooper at the jump bay.

"Go" is the last word a paratrooper hears from the jumpmaster as he clears the jump bay.

Infantry troops in Vietnam in a heavily vegetated area. (NARA archives).

5. Gear
5.1. Headgear

US Army paratroopers did not wear any distinctive headgear as airborne troops, but wore the same service and utility caps as any other infantry unit. The only exception regarding headgear was the M1 helmet, of which a special version was made for paratroopers: the M1C. When their parachute opened, the standard M1 helmet tended to tilt backwards, making it liable to be lost or injuring the soldier in the nape of the neck. This problem was solved with the M1C.

A member of Company B, 2nd Brigade, 82nd Airborne Division, prepares for a troop drop during an exercise in August, 1977.

M1C Parachutist's Helmet

The M1 helmet had an innovative design that was the result of studies by the US Army Research Team at Fort Benning in 1940. It was adopted in 1941 throughout the US Armed Services to replace the M1917A1, inspired on the British helmet in use during that period. The M1 had novel features such as a lower profile, rather than the earlier wide brim, giving enhanced protection to the ears and nape. In addition to this, it had a double structure with a steel exterior complemented by an inner fiber layer that supported the suspension system. It was manufactured in one size and was therefore quite large, and was fitted to the soldier's head with the interior retention and suspension system.

M1 helmet in the paratrooper configuration, with the "Mitchell pattern" camo cover. The identification tapes, shown here in white, were used for the drop in Operation Junction City.

In the early days, paratroopers trained with close-fitting fiber helmets similar to those used in football. When the M1 model was adopted, with its large size and high resistance to the air during descent, paratroopers received a specially designed version that allowed it to be securely fastened to prevent it from being lost during the jump. It was named M1C, and the difference lay solely in the retention straps on both the steel shell and the fiber liner. On the ground, soldiers normally wore the additional straps concealed in the helmet liner to keep them out of the way, which made the helmet look identical to the M1 worn by the infantry.

The M1 helmet was redesigned over the following decades, in models 1958, 1964 and 1972, but the special paratrooper version was maintained practically unchanged with regard to the retention system. From 1959, the US Army issued a camouflage cover for the M1. This Mitchell Pattern used previously by the Marines Corps for their tents in 1953, featured a reversible pattern in shades of green and leaf shapes on one side, and mottled brown on the other. This cover remained in general use until the mid-seventies, when it was replaced by the camo cover in the same design as the troops' uniforms. The M1 helmet was kept in service until the mid-eighties, when the PASGT helmet was issued, manufactured in Kevlar, a synthetic material with ballistic qualities.

M1C Parachutist's Helmet Shell

In 1941 the steel helmet was manufactured from Hadfield Manganese Steel plate, with a weight of 2.25 pounds and an antimagnetic stainless steel rim. Rectangular bales, also made of stainless steel, were fitted on each side to which the chinstrap was attached. In October 1944 the stainless steel rim was replaced by an anti-reflection rim in the same material as the helmet.

The M1 helmet bore markings (numbers and letters) on the inside of the front visor, with a heat treatment stamp, to identify the production lot.

The earliest chinstraps were sewn onto the bales. On the left side, this had a piece of steel wire ended in a double hook, while the strap on the right, adjustable in length, ended in a rectangular buckle to receive the hook. In addition, from the middle of 1944, a new ball hook release was added to the right-hand-side fastener. This would automatically release the chinstrap under pressure in close combat freeing the helmet and preventing neck injuries. This buckle was called the T1 and included a newly designed stamped metal hook for the left strap.

In the 1950s, the strap was fixed to the helmet by a metal piece that hooked onto the swivel bale. The chinstraps were made of ¾ inch wide cotton web, commonly worn in Vietnam fastened on the rear of the helmet.

During parachute jumps there is a high risk of troopers' helmets falling off and being lost. The M1C incorporated an extension on the chinstrap with a snap hook (the male snap) that attached to inner lining, keeping the shell and liner together more effectively. To this end, the liner has a female snap. In the first model, issued in 1942, the helmet shell had a fixed bale in a D-shape, and was called M2. After December 1944 the D-bale was discontin-

ued, in favor of a standard swivel bale and the helmet was renamed M1C.

Helmet manufacture was stepped up for the Vietnam War, and a million were produced between 1966 and 1967. These later helmets presented a reduced profile, with a less pronounced dome shape. They were painted with a sand texture in a characteristic Light Olive Green or Lime Green color, rather than the darker shades of green (OD319) used for helmets in the fifties.

From 1955, the liner for helmet M1C consisted of merely adding the inverted-A sidepieces to the chinstrap, to the sides of the liner, sometimes without sharing the suspension system retention points. The changes made to the M1 in 1972, that affected both the suspension system and the chinstrap, were not applied to the M1C, which remained unchanged since 1966.

M1C Parachutist's Helmet Liner

The liners were made of plastic fibers –laminated nylon from 1958– and were given the appropriate shape to fit inside the shell. Generally speaking, the exterior of the liner was painted in the same green color as the helmet shell, but with a much smoother texture. The interior, however, was unpainted and the brown and black construction fibers were visible.

The suspension system around the liner was secured with six semi-tubular rivets and steel or brass A-shaped washers. The headband was attached to the suspension and was adjustable to any size head. Another component, the neckband,

covered the nape and kept the helmet steady on the wearer's head. In 1964 certain changes were made in the construction of the liner. The neckband became hexagonal in shape and attached to the liner via three adjustable straps, while the leather chinstrap –typical of earlier models– was eliminated.

WWII paratroopers' helmet liners had an additional chincup that held the helmet firmly to the chin. It was made of leather and was joined to the sides of the liner by means of webbing straps in an inverted A shape with buckles at the apex. Later, this leather chincup was replaced by another model manu-

factured in cotton web with metal grommets. On the models issued in 1958 and 1964 the A-strap system was maintained, but since 1964 it was riveted independently from the suspension system. For a jump, the regulations state that paratroopers must secure both helmet shell and liner chinstraps. The helmet shell chinstrap must be threaded through the horizontal bar of the A-strap to hold the helmet more securely in place. After landing, the liner chinstrap was usually stowed in the interior using only the helmet shell chinstrap, although soldiers would often be seen wearing the liner chinstrap because the chincup gave better helmet stability.

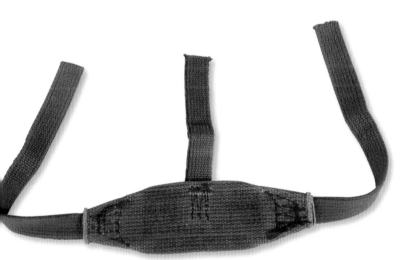

The neckstrap helped to secure the helmet to the head, and carried item data printed on the inside.

Parachutist helmet chincup and detail of the stitching between the metal eyelets, characteristic of pre-1980 items.

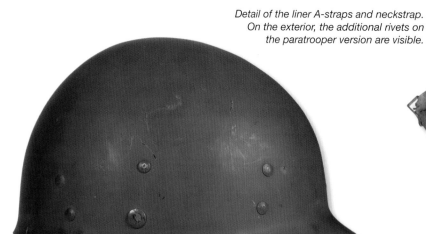

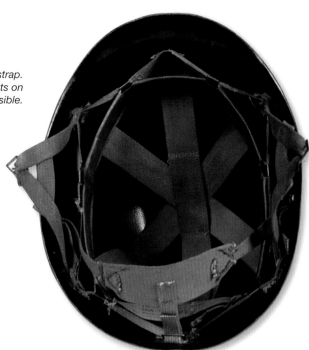

Detail of the liner A-straps and neckstrap. On the exterior, the additional rivets on the paratrooper version are visible.

Interior markings on the liner indicate the manufacturer and the year, in this case 1968.

The markings in this liner tell us it was made in 1971.

The construction of this paratrooper helmet (unpainted) liner can be seen, consisting of fine layers of fabric and resin.

PFC James E. Stadig and other members of Co D, 2nd Bn, 35th Inf, 3rd Bde, 4th Inf [...] come out of a cave after checking it for Viet Cong men or equipment during a one day sea[...] and destroy mission in the Quang Ngai Province, 8 km west of Duc Pho. (NARA archive[...]

The latest helmet liners were made of thicker and more flexible material.

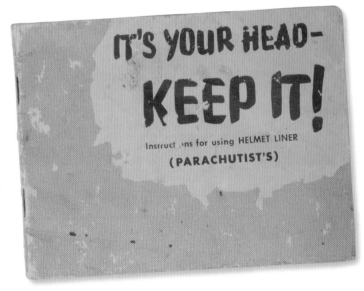

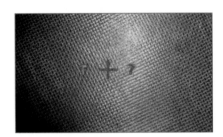

Interior markings on a liner manufactured by Firestone.

The handbook "It's your head - Keep it!" for the M1 helmet in its paratrooper version contained instructions for use.

5.2. Uniforms

Work and Field Uniforms were soldiers' everyday clothing, particularly when performing physical tasks at the barracks and on field activities, and also their battledress uniforms. During the Cold War years, these were the Utility uniforms, that we remember as the typical olive drab shirt and trousers worn by American soldiers at their US headquarters and bases abroad. For south-east Asia, the Tropical uniform was adapted to the needs of soldiers in combat which included greater carrying capacity, in lighter, more breathable fabric for the tropical climate

conditions. In this category there were also uniforms made of woolen cloth and the field jackets and trousers worn by troops in cold weather, both at the barracks and during field training.

Paratroopers were considered as infantry and received the same equipment as the rest of army units. Their uniforms were not adapted to jumping from aircraft, and they jumped wearing the same clothes as their colleagues on the ground, according to the time of year and the barracks regulations, so they could wear the utility uniform by

itself or with a field jacket for the cold. During the 1970s, owing to the demands of the fight in Vietnam, the US Army implemented a succession of changes to soldiers' uniforms. This process took them from the uniforms of the post-war period in the 1950s, to uniforms featuring many improvements and designs whose origins were twofold: on the one hand, experience and, to a large extent, adapting to the war situation in south-eastern Asia; and on the other hand, as a result of breakthroughs in technology by US industries and military laboratories.

Utility Uniform

The Utility Uniform had smaller pocket space, but its simplicity permitted other garments to be worn over it in cold climate conditions.

The Utility Uniform was composed of a shirt with two patch pockets on the chest, and trousers with front and rear flat pockets, providing limited carrying capacity. This had evolved from those used by American troops in WWII and Korea. It was adopted in 1952 as the US Army uniform, although it was not produced at that time in sufficient quantities to be used in combat in the Korean War.

The Utility Uniform was made of a new 8.5 oz. cotton sateen fabric, twice as durable as the previous HBT (Herringbone Twill) material, in Olive Green shade 107 (OG-107). In addition, its design was simpler. In the first 1952 version, the shirt had two patch pockets on the chest (the left pocket had a pencil holder), with rectangular flaps, and the sleeves were tubular, without cuffs or buttons. The front closure was a single row of unconcealed plastic buttons.

Straight flaps on the pockets were characteristic of the first model of Utility Shirt.

Flat hip and rear pockets were a typical feature on all models of Utility Trousers.

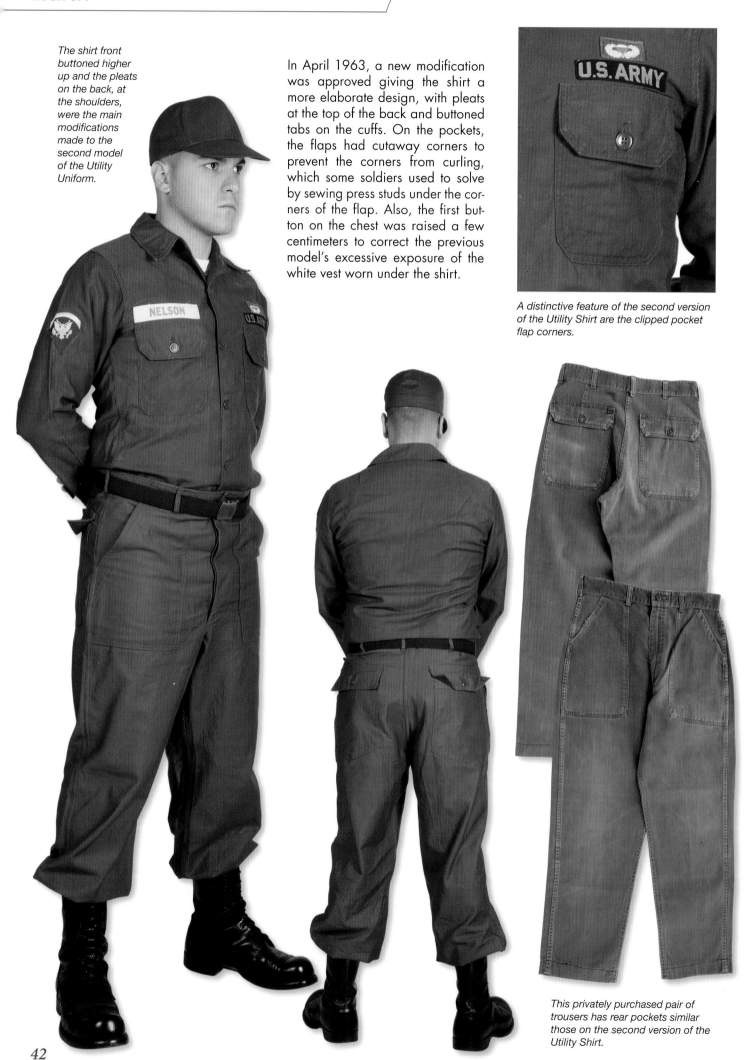

The shirt front buttoned higher up and the pleats on the back, at the shoulders, were the main modifications made to the second model of the Utility Uniform.

In April 1963, a new modification was approved giving the shirt a more elaborate design, with pleats at the top of the back and buttoned tabs on the cuffs. On the pockets, the flaps had cutaway corners to prevent the corners from curling, which some soldiers used to solve by sewing press studs under the corners of the flap. Also, the first button on the chest was raised a few centimeters to correct the previous model's excessive exposure of the white vest worn under the shirt.

A distinctive feature of the second version of the Utility Shirt are the clipped pocket flap corners.

This privately purchased pair of trousers has rear pockets similar those on the second version of the Utility Shirt.

The third model of utility uniform appeared in November 1964. With the purpose of standardizing uniform apparel across all the services, it was adopted by the US Army, Marines, Navy and Air Force. By the mid-sixties it became customary for the Marines, but in the Army, owing to the large stocks of the earlier version, it was common to see soldiers wearing all three models combined. In this third model, the back pleats disappeared from the shirt and the sleeves gained buttoned cuffs. The other main visible difference were the chest pockets with pointed flaps. Furthermore, toward 1967, the flat buttons were replaced by the conical buttons already in used on jungle uniforms.

The Utility Trousers were designed on a simple pattern with straight legs and no cargo pockets on the leg. The trousers issued in 1952 were made of the same material as the shirt, and had two front patch pockets and two more, with flaps, on the rear, a row of buttons on the

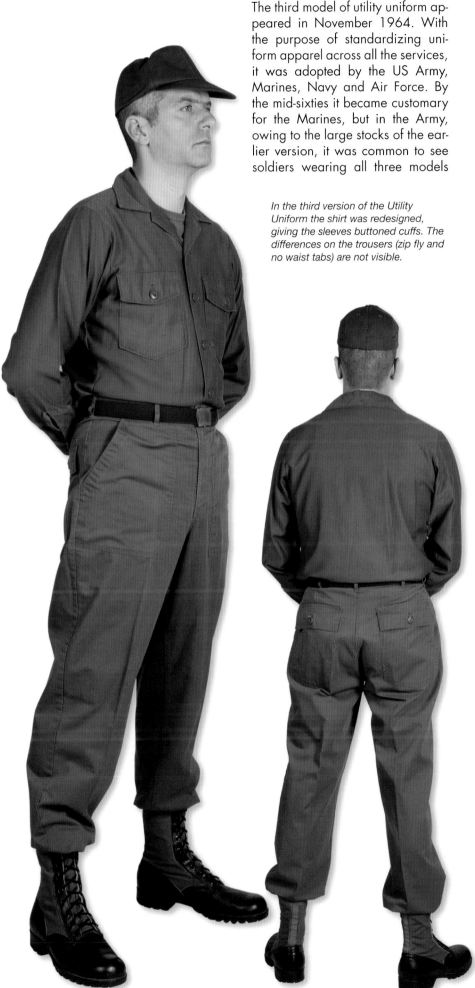

In the third version of the Utility Uniform the shirt was redesigned, giving the sleeves buttoned cuffs. The differences on the trousers (zip fly and no waist tabs) are not visible.

The V-shaped pocket flap is typical to the third version of the Utility Shirt. Concave buttons replaced the earlier flat buttons.

fly and side waistband adjustment tabs. After the utility uniform was modified in 1963 the trousers were altered slightly, and the waist tabs were eliminated.

In the airborne units, authorization was given to wear modified trousers, that could be bought at barracks outlets, with two flat side pockets similar to the patch pockets on the shirt. However, this was more to do with differentiation than with increasing cargo capacity.

American troops in Vietnam wore the Utility Uniform from the early days in the country. The Military Assistance and Advisory Group-Vietnam (MAAG-Vietnam) had 700 advisors in 1960, a figure that had increased to 24,000 by 1964, in diverse support roles to the South Vietnamese armed forces. Though from 1963 the new tropical uniform was tested, issued to the Special Forces in south-east Asia, the first combat troops sent to Vietnam wore the same Utility Uniforms worn at home, and the first battles in the country were fought in this uniform. These were subsequently replaced with the Tropical Uniform as it became available, but utilities remained in service with the rear-guard troops up to end of the conflict.

In the paratrooper units, soldiers were allowed to wear trousers with side cargo pockets.

In Vietnam rules were made for wearing utilities that were contrary to the general regulations, such as wearing the shirt outside the trousers or rolling up the sleeves. These were called for by the need to endure the intense heat of the tropical climate, and soldiers carrying out heavy physical work, such as engineers, were even allowed to remove their shirts and even their T-shirt.

These pants were modified versions of the Utility Trousers or garments privately acquired at the base PX stores.

Infantry troops crossing a river near An Khe, South Vietnam, in October 1965.

Tropical Uniform

Tropical Uniform, third model, made of rip-stop poplin.

Known as "jungle fatigues", the Tropical Uniform was the most famous uniform in this war. It was invented for this war, and was made of cool, lightweight fabric, and the garments were loose fitting for comfort and to allow air to circulate: an important aspect in an environment where, as well as one's own perspiration, frequent rains and an abundance of waterways caused clothing to be wet. Moreover, in this kind of warfare, spending long periods in the field, maximum cargo capacity was needed and the Tropical Uniform had spacious pockets on the jacket and the trousers. In addition, to protect uniforms from getting torn on the sharp undergrowth, the new "rip-stop" material was developed which gave fabric greater resistance without affecting its other properties.

With thousands of American advisors in south-east Asia, in October 1962 the Quartermaster Research and Engineering Command was requested to develop a uniform suited to the conditions under which the Special Forces were operating in Vietnam. The uniform, adopted in mid-1963, was inspired on model M-1942 used by WWII paratroopers. It was called Tropical Combat Coat and Trousers and was manufactured in 5.5 oz. Wind-Resistant Cotton Poplin OG-107.

The first version of the tropical coat had four large front gusset pockets with drainage holes. The top pockets were slanted to give easier access to their contents, and had an interior pencil compartment. The coat could be fitted to the body with the waist adjustment tabs. The

The capacious slant pockets are a characteristic of the Tropical Uniform.

front double closure ("gas flap") kept chemical agents out and gave extra protection against wind and insects. Shoulder tabs were provided on this item of clothing, as on the field jackets, but which had been removed from the utility uniforms.

As chief differentiating feature with regard to future variations, all the pockets have simple flaps; buttoned down, the glossy dark green buttons remain in view.

Over the next few years a long series of modifications took place, with some mixed features in progressing from one pattern to another. The second variation of the Tropical Uniform appeared in 1965, resulting from the experience gathered during the first months of usage in Vietnam. The main modification was to conceal the buttons on all pockets with double flaps to prevent them from snagging on the undergrowth.

By this time, the first US Army combat troops were arriving in Vietnam, such as the 173rd Airborne

US infantry on a Tree Days Search and Destroy Operation, near Bien Hoa, scouting for enemy activity in August 1965.

Brigade or the 101st Airborne Division, followed shortly after by the 1st Cavalry Division, the 1st Infantry Division and the 25th Infantry Division before the end of 1965. They all arrived with four sets of the utility uniform, and were provided with their tropical uniforms at the Central Issue Facility at Long Binh. However, tropical uniform issue was slow and, despite being a priority for the infantry units, by year's end soldiers were still fighting in a combination of items from the Tropical Uniform and the Utility Uniform.

During the period 1966-1967 a series of modifications gave rise to the third Tropical Jacket model. The shoulder tabs, waist adjustment tabs and gas flap were removed, which made it easier to manufacture and freed it from some bothersome details, that would get caught in the harness or would cause discomfort from buttons pressing into the soldier's skin under heavy packs.

By the end of 1967, the poplin fabric was further developed with a new design incorporating an internal crosshatch of stronger threads that prevents ripping and tearing, called "Wind-Resistant Rip-stop Cotton Poplin OG-107". From then, the

tropical uniform design remained almost unchanged up to the end of the war in Vietnam.

The Tropical Trousers featured two front pockets, two rear pockets and two large cargo pockets on the thighs. They had a button fly and were adjusted at the waist with button tabs. In the first version, the pocket buttons were visible and the hip pockets had a vertical opening. A tape deployed from the interior of the cargo pockets could be used to secure the pocket to the leg, to avoid the contents from swinging.

The trousers were worn bloused, over the bootlegs, and were equipped with a tape to tie them in that position.

In the second version of the trousers, the buttons on the pockets were concealed and the opening on the front pockets was slanted. Later, in the third version, the waist tab was replaced with a tape with a metal fastener, which allowed up to 4 inches adjustment in size, and the securing tape was eliminated from the cargo pockets. In addition, greater flexibility was given at the knee with a tuck and, later, the button fly was replaced with a zip fly.

George Mason, Infantryman in Vietnam, wears the Tropical Uniform and the LCE M1956 on which several grenades are suspended.

ERDL Tropical Uniform

In 1948, the Army Engineer Research and Development Laboratories (ERDL) began to develop a new four-color camouflage pattern. The base color was Yellow Green army shade 354, on which Brown army shade 356 and Dark Green army shade 355 were added in an 'amoeba' design. Black army shade 357 is added in the form of irregular, stylized shadows.

The ERDL camouflage in lime-dominant colors for the Tropical Uniform was designed for forest conditions.

With a camouflage uniform, the purpose is for the colors to blend into the background terrain, while the contrasting colors cause the camouflage to break up the image maintaining its effectiveness over a greater distance. The results obtained from the studies carried out showed that the difference between brown and green was effective at distances of up to 100 m, while the light-dark differentiation was effective up to 200 m.

In November 1965 discussions took place over the need to issue the tropical uniform in camouflage colors, but a negative conclusion was reached in spite of several hundred ERDL camouflage uniforms having been sent to Vietnam for assessment in the field, distributed to Recce units. Following this assessment, in February 1967, US Army Vietnam (USARV) made an initial order of some 20,000 uniforms for Recce teams: Pathfinders, LRRPs (Long Range Reconnaissance Patrol), Scout/Recon and Special Forces. By the middle of the year, the ERDL was adopted as standard for the selected units, but did not begin to arrive in Vietnam until the end of the year.

The ERDL camouflage pattern was adopted, from 1967, for the third version of the Tropical Uniform.

Tropical Uniform in ERDL brown-dominant camouflage for mountain conditions.

The ERDL tropical uniform was manufactured in 1967 in the poplin material used for the third model and, as the tropical uniform evolved, so did its camo version, so that at any time it was made in the same version as the Olive Green 107. In 1968 it was manufactured from the new rip-stop poplin. These uniforms came in two variants. One was designed for lowlands, and the predominant base color was yellowish –known as "lime-dominant"– and adopted as the initial ERDL color scheme.

The other ERDL camo variant was known as "brown dominant" and was intended for mountain terrain, in predominantly brown shades, with a brown base marked with darker browns and greens.

After the Vietnam War, the ERDL camouflage fabric was used to make uniforms for marines, paratroopers and rangers in what was known as the transitional model (due to the fact that it was manufactured until the appearance of the BDU uniform in Woodland camouflage in the early eighties) or the RDF model, because it was distributed to the units in the Rapid Deployment Force.

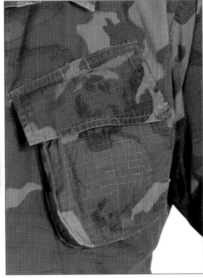

The breast pocket has a pencil holder.

The gusset pockets provide greater cargo capacity.

5.3. Footgear

For soldiers preparing to jump from an airplane, the risk of injury from landing with their feet in unknown terrain is very high. To increase paratroopers' safety they were issued special footgear. However, in view of the fact that in Vietnam airborne units acted as infantry troops, they were equipped with tropical boots, specially designed for the warm and humid climate conditions in the area.

Paratrooper Leather Boots

From the outset, paratroopers have sought to distinguish themselves from the rest, and to underscore the rigorous training they undergo and the additional risk they take in jumping from aircraft. One of the most iconic elements for paratroopers are their jump boots. Their design began in 1940, specifically for parachutists. The prototypes were tested by the units that were being trained at that time, and the first model, adopted in August 1942, was designated "Boots, Jumper, Parachute".

Jump boots were made of brown leather. The boots had a high shaft and fitted closely at the ankles. The overall height was 10 inches, and they had front laces with two rows of 12 or 13 eyelets. The shaft was reinforced on the exterior at the rear quarter, and the high toe also had an extra layer giving it greater resistance and its characteristic appearance. Stitching was four-ply at the seams and the ankles were protected by a web band sewn inside the boot. The soles were rubber and divided in two separate parts, sewn and nailed. A peculiarity is that the heel was tilted on the inside, to prevent the boot from getting caught by protruding gear or cables on the aircraft floor before a jump.

One of the leading jump boots manufacturers was Corcoran, and this name has remained as a synonym for jump boots.

Since brown leather items were changed to black in 1956, jump boots were also issued in black and the brown stocks were dyed black in 1958, compliant with the regulation.

Corcoran Boots adapted closely to the foot. They have rounded toe and stitching at the heels.

As opposed to the Infantry's Combat Boots, Corcoran Boots had two-piece rubber soles.

1965 commercial for Corcoran Jump Boots in the "Airborne Quarterly" paratroopers' magazine.

Jump boots became so famous that they were soldiers' preferred footwear. In the 1940s and during the Korean War, all soldiers hoped to get a pair of jump boots instead of model M1943 with side buckles. The Army decided to replace these with a new model of boot, the M1948, which were very similar to the jump boots; nevertheless, paratroopers and the Special Forces continued to wear jump boots as a distinctive feature.

The status symbol value reached by jump boots was so great that airborne troops were authorized to wear their duty uniform, such as the Army Green uniform and the Khaki uniform, with jump boots instead of shoes, and their trousers bloused over them.

The line of perforations on the toe is a feature of this boot model.

The manufacturer, Corcoran, could also be identified by the letter C under the heel.

Inner Corcoran brand tag.

Tropical Boots

As already shown in the war in the Pacific, it became clear in Vietnam that adequate boots were necessary for combat in a tropical environment and to move in the jungle. They had to be resistant against water, mud, soft terrain, the heat, insects, leeches, etc.

At the end of WWII a model of jungle boots was adopted that had developed from the experience of wars in Asia and the Pacific. Their design was based on the leather M1943 combat boots, but with a canvas shank to make then lighter and cooler, and with traction soles.

In the early 1960s some troops in Vietnam were issued jungle boots, nicknamed "Okinawa boots" when many advisors were given these boots with their tropical gear in Okinawa, before their departure

1st Model

Tropical Boots, first model, designed for use in Vietnam.

for Vietnam. However, they had stitched soles, and tended to come unstitched when the sun and humidity rotted the seams. Another hitch were the buckles, a legacy from model M1943, which snagged on equipment and jungle undergrowth.

A new model of tropical boot was therefore proposed, which began to be developed in 1955 and incorporated every technological advance. The most notable was the vulcanization system for soles, making stitching unnecessary and sealing the sole to the rest of the boot. The Direct Molded Sole (DMS) system consisted in modeling the sole and the heel in a single piece built directly onto the boot with a high-pressure vulcanization method. For the tread, the classic model used on European mountaineering boots known as the Vibram pattern was adopted. The result was a leather boot with a rubber sole, and a canvas shank with laces. The shank was made of olive green nylon/cotton canvas, and the boots were issued with insert soles of plastic fiber mesh PVDC (Saran) with low moisture and odor absorbency, and that favored air circulation through the ventilation eyelets in the sides of the boots.

The early Tropical Boots versions included a fabric label with information on the item name and military contract. Pictured is an item made under a 1964 contract.

The size, 9 Regular, and the manufacturing date, November 1963, are shown on the leather reinforcement.

Leather boot shaft reinforcements were standard on the first Tropical Boot version.

Insert soles allow air to circulate inside the boot.

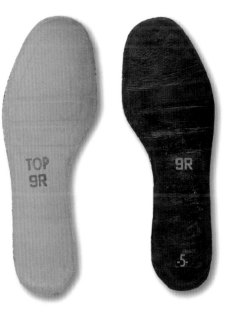

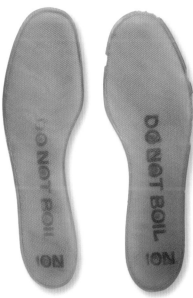

Initially, the insert soles had a metal plate to give protection against sharp booby traps.

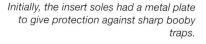

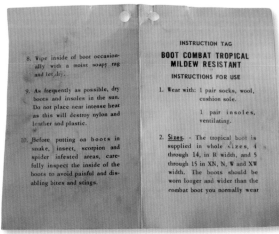

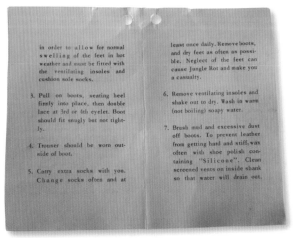

Tropical Boots were issued with an instructions leaflet.

A second version of tropical boots brought some modifications such as the use of nylon supports in the shaft instead of the original leather reinforcements, and the adoption of a steel plate inside the soles to provide protection from sharp traps set by the enemy in Vietnam. Later, in a third version, ankle reinforcements were added.

2nd Model

Fabric label with the item name, military contract and size.

The folded seam at the base of the heel is present in all models of Tropical Boots.

The insert soles were made of a dirt-repellent material.

3rd Model

Vibram soles featured deep treads for a better grip.

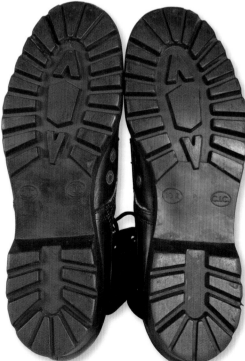

In 1966, in the area around the Panama Canal, at the headquarters of the US Army School of the Americas for jungle warfare, a new sole was developed that would shed mud while walking and thus maintain traction. This design, with wide transversal and longitudinal lugs, was also tested in Vietnam with satisfactory results and in April 1968 it was ordered that Panama soles would replace Vibram soles on tropical boots.

4ᵗʰ Model

The second version of Tropical Boots incorporated nylon reinforcements.

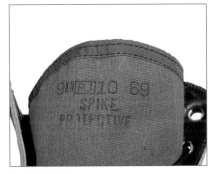

With the addition of a metal plate to the soles, the boots were called "Spike protective."

The data on this label was printed directly onto the tongue. The boot shown is size 10 Narrow, manufactured in March 1968.

Panama soles were designed to shed mud when walking.

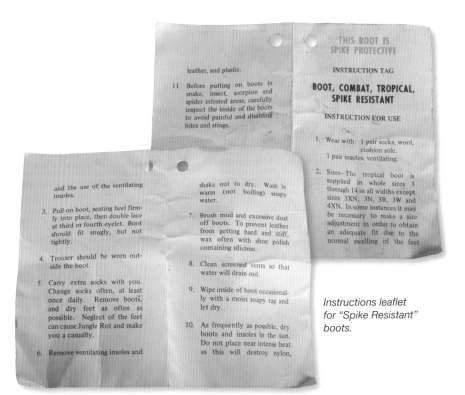

Instructions leaflet for "Spike Resistant" boots.

5.4. Individual Combat Equipment

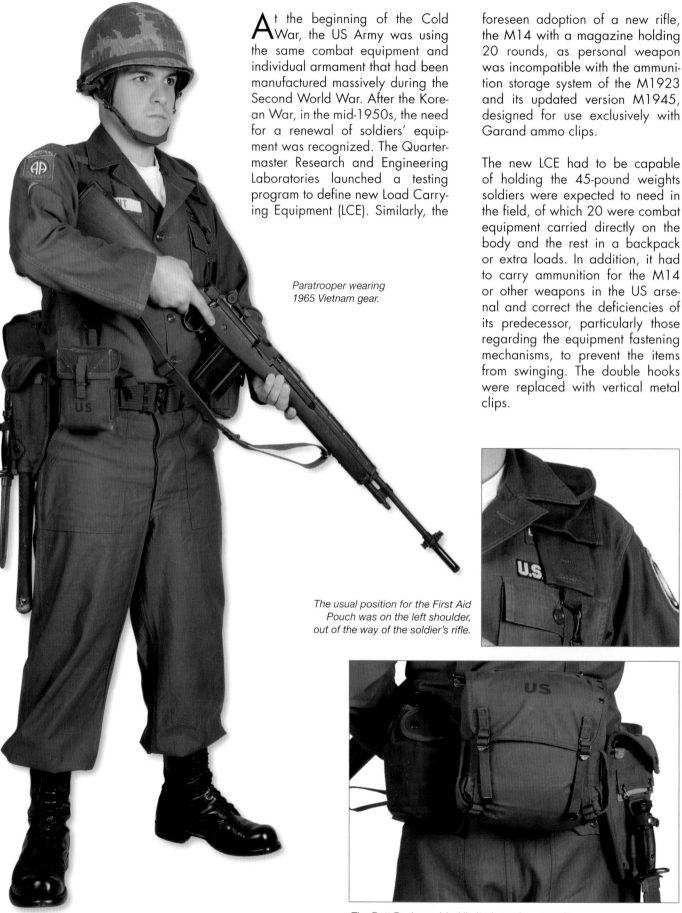

At the beginning of the Cold War, the US Army was using the same combat equipment and individual armament that had been manufactured massively during the Second World War. After the Korean War, in the mid-1950s, the need for a renewal of soldiers' equipment was recognized. The Quartermaster Research and Engineering Laboratories launched a testing program to define new Load Carrying Equipment (LCE). Similarly, the foreseen adoption of a new rifle, the M14 with a magazine holding 20 rounds, as personal weapon was incompatible with the ammunition storage system of the M1923 and its updated version M1945, designed for use exclusively with Garand ammo clips.

The new LCE had to be capable of holding the 45-pound weights soldiers were expected to need in the field, of which 20 were combat equipment carried directly on the body and the rest in a backpack or extra loads. In addition, it had to carry ammunition for the M14 or other weapons in the US arsenal and correct the deficiencies of its predecessor, particularly those regarding the equipment fastening mechanisms, to prevent the items from swinging. The double hooks were replaced with vertical metal clips.

Paratrooper wearing 1965 Vietnam gear.

The usual position for the First Aid Pouch was on the left shoulder, out of the way of the soldier's rifle.

The Butt Pack provided limited carrying capacity.

In March 1957 the new equipment was adopted with the denomination M1956 ILCE (Individual Load Carrying Equipment). In its Combat or Fighting Load versions, the M1956 comprised the basic items of fighting gear and weighed, with the weapon and ammunition, around 40 pounds. In the Full Field or Existence Load versions, a further 20 pounds were added in clothing, a poncho, a sleeping bag and the gas mask.

The essential components of the M1956 equipment were the pistol belt, the suspenders, two ammunition pouches, a first aid or compass pouch, a canteen cover, an entrenching tool carrier, a sleeping bag carrier and a butt pack. All these items were manufactured in Dark Olive Green cotton webbing with black oxidized brass, steel or alloy for buckles, keepers, eyelets and other metal parts. The kit was assembled in a given order as established in the regulations to ensure that the weight was evenly distributed, in such a manner that when the soldier unfastened the belt, it remained in balance and the load did not fall to one side. This was especially important for paratroopers who, when donning their parachutes and during their descent, wore their pistol belt open so that the ammo pouches moved to the sides and did not interfere with the harness and reserve parachute.

As during WWII, cotton canvas equipment was found to have many drawbacks in a tropical climate owing to its high water absorption capacity, increasing its weight by 40% when wet, and that its slow drying rate favored the growth of mold. Furthermore, after repeated saturation and drying the material deteriorated and lost its properties.

Halfway through the conflict, late items from the M1956 design were the most common.

In Vietnam, it was ruled that each soldier should carry two water canteens, on account of the tropical conditions.

The army researched new materials such as aluminum and nylon, which had an absorbency of just 8%, dried rapidly and was more abrasion resistant, to improve equipment performance. In addition, this material was lighter and reduced the weight of the M1956 from five pounds to just three. However, it had its detractors, too, who claimed it was more uncomfortable due to its greater rigidity, tended to have a shiny finish, made more noise and could produce severe burns if ignited.

The first prototypes appeared in the mid-1960s, and in 1967 they were sent to south-east Asia for evaluation. The results of the trials were satisfactory and in 1968 an order was

placed for 200,000 units of nylon equipment known as Modernized Load Carrying Equipment (MLCE) M1967 for troops in Vietnam. Supplies were irregular and the new kit was not issued as a whole but as separate items, as these became available. This meant that the new items were generally used mixed with the canvas M1956 equipment.

The M1967 equipment never fully replaced the cotton canvas kit, but research was pursued and by the end of North American intervention in Vietnam a new outfit of equipment had been designed, called the All-purpose Lightweight Individual Carrying Equipment (ALICE) M1972, and was issued from the mid-1970s.

During a rest in their company area at Lai Khe, South Vietnam, soldiers pile their kit on the ground.

Pistol Belt

Initially, at the turn of the 20th century, the Pistol Belt was adapted to the requirements of the Colt M1911 pistol and became the basis for gun belts in the next decades. In 1936 it was modified, and under the new denomination Belt, Pistol or Revolver M1936 remained in use through the 1940s and 50s. This belt was made of 11-strand horizontal weave cotton webbing with a quick-fastening brass buckle. The belt had three rows of metal eyelets

along its length. The middle row was for adjusting the belt length and the outside rows were to hook on suspenders or hang from them other items of equipment fitted with a double hook to insert into the eyelets. Two vertical keepers helped to secure the end of the adjustable belt.

During WWII the pistol belt was only issued to soldiers equipped with a pistol or carbine, but was authorized after the war for all parachute troops, who carried Garand rifle ammo clips in the M1 carbine magazine pouches instead of using the M1923 Cartridge Belt. From the pistol belt they carried suspenders and the rest of their kit.

With the LCE M1956 a new Pistol Belt was adopted, similar to its predecessor, adjustable at both ends and featuring a new brass buckle with a ball or button fastening in-

Vertical weave Pistol Belt. The closure system on the M1956 Pistol Belt was ball-type, easier to handle than the earlier T-type.

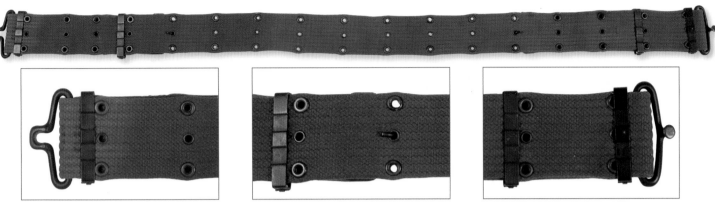

Horizontal weave Pistol Belt M1956. The sliding keepers are designed to run easily over the three rows of eyelets.

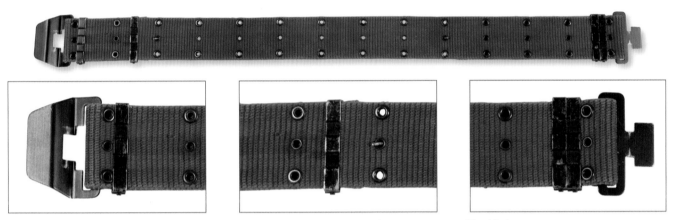

The Davis quick-release mechanism was also used on cotton canvas Pistol Belts.

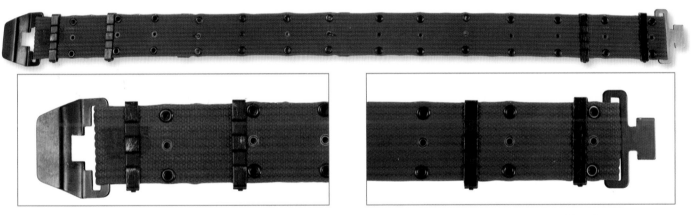

The Davis quick-release mechanism never replaced the previous model due to its tendency to open accidentally.

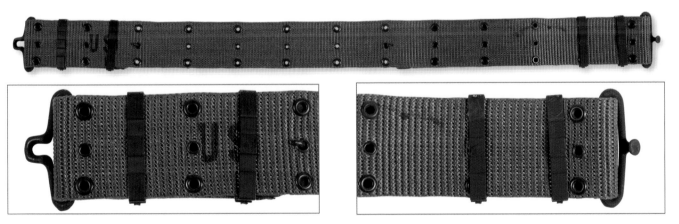

The M1967 Pistol Belt was made of vertical weave nylon.

stead of the T-fastener on model M1923, which rendered it easier to put on and take off. Later, in 1966, vertical weave webbing was used, rather than horizontal, giving it more resistance and stiffness, as it had a tendency to lose its shape, particularly in the environmental conditions in Vietnam.

With the M1967 nylon combat equipment, the vertical weave nylon belt had an aluminium buckle developed by Davis Aircraft,

with a T-hook at one end and a quick-release flange at the other. It was soon found that this buckle was prone to opening accidentally, hence it was not used extensively and the nylon belt was issued either with the Davis buckle or the standard model M1956 buckle. The new Davis buckle was also issued with some belts in the cotton model M1956, although this did not become generalized owing to the detected problems.

The buckle was marked with the manufacturer's data.

Suspenders

Left to right: M1956 suspenders, first and second versions, and M1967 nylon suspenders.

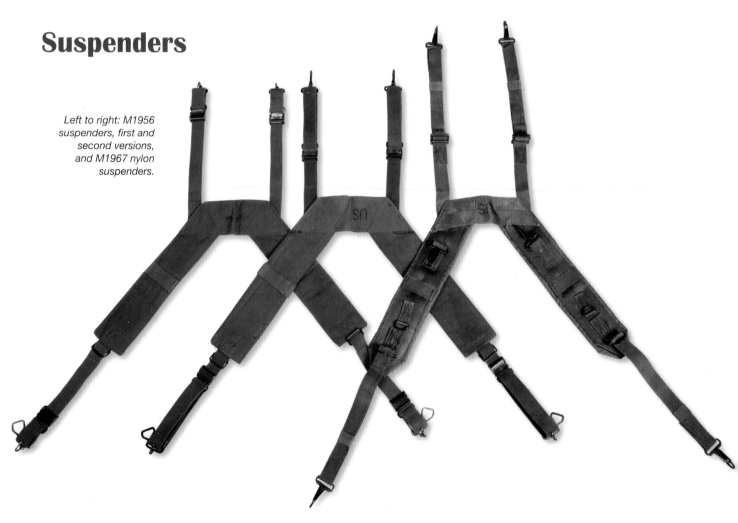

The suspenders help to support the loads secured to the belt, and at the same time serve to secure further items of the soldier's kit. Suspenders, Field Pack, Combat, M1956 were known as 'H-suspenders' because of their shape. The straps were adjustable in length with metal keepers, and ended in hooks that could be inserted in the top row of eyelets on the belt, in front, and to the field pack at the back. In the case of a paratrooper

ready for a jump, the suspenders were lengthened to the maximum allowing the belt to rest below the waist. Additionally, they attached directly onto the belt, causing the field pack to rest in a lower position where it would not interfere with the parachute pack tray. At the top of the front straps was a rectangular metal loop on which to secure straps for several other items of gear. It was also useful for hanging a torch, or hand grenades simply

by hooking the 'spoon' through the loop. Furthermore, the shoulder pads had two crosspieces to which equipment could be fastened, and where the sleeping bag carrier and the pack adapter were secured.

The MLCE M1967 suspenders still had the H shape, but came in a single size. The four adjustable straps were now long enough to adapt to any height. The straps ended in a newly designed hook, with a

The first M-1956 model had welded wire hooks.

On the second M-1956 version, the hooks were replaced with the standard hook from earlier models on the back and a stamped metal hook on the front.

The M-1967 suspenders featured new hooks with a quick-release mechanism.

protective cover to prevent it from catching unexpectedly.

The front rings on the shoulder pad were moved to a higher position

and two hooks were added to hold the field pack without needing an adapter, which was dropped from the kit. Nevertheless, these hooks were just above the shoulder

and some soldiers found them a nuisance because they tended to get caught on other straps, and indeed they disappeared from the next design, the M1972 ALICE.

Field Pack

The Field Pack appeared with the M1956 equipment, replacing the previous Combat Pack. This was a small rucksack that attached to the belt in the lumbar region, which is why it was better known as the "Butt pack" or "Fanny pack". Its purpose was to carry a day's rations and the necessary kit for field operations, such as underwear, socks and toiletries.

Field Pack M1956, shaped like a rectangular box.

The M1956 Field Pack was a single compartment bag closed with a flap. As well as the interior contents, equipment could also be carried on the outside thanks to a system of loops, straps and eyelets. For instance, a field jacket or

poncho could be strapped under the flap, or with straps provided underneath. It was also common practice to hang canteens or the E-tool from the sides. On the initial version, M1956, two side flaps in addition to the main flap pro-

tected the rucksack contents. On the back, it had two keepers for fastening the pack to the belt, and two eyelets to join it to the rear suspender straps.

A second improved version of the Field Pack appeared in 1961, called Pack, Field, M1961. This new pack had increased capacity, being wider, and better waterproofing thanks to a lining of rubber coated fabric at the opening.

Field Pack M1961 increased load capacity and was more rounded in shape.

The Adaptor, Pack, Field M1956 was an accessory for raising the field pack fastening high up on the soldier's back. This freed up space lower down to accommodate more load on the pistol belt, or to prevent the pack from getting wet on crossing a river.

This Adapter allowed the Field Pack to be carried higher on the soldier's back.

Test-firing at Phuoc-Vinh, South Vietnam. The men carry the LCE M1956 and are using M16 assault rifles and M79 grenade launchers.

The use of field packs was more common during the early years of the war, but their capacity was insufficient for the soldiers' needs in field operations and they were substituted by larger backpacks.

In the nylon MLCE M1967 equipment, the field pack was almost identical to the cotton canvas M1961, but with a few differences in design. It was envisaged that when worn in a high position, it would be attached directly to the dedicated hooks at the top of the suspenders. For that reason, it also had two straps with metal snaps to secure it to the suspenders back straps and prevent the field pack from swinging.

Field Pack M1967 was similar to M1961, but made of nylon.

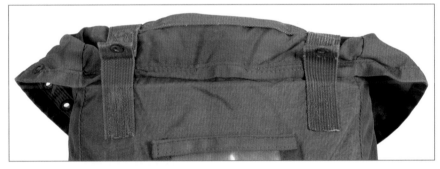

The eyelets for suspenders are typical of model M1967, used during the sixties, and were replaced with D-rings in the years after the Vietnam War.

The MLCE M1967 included the field pack for testing in Vietnam. However, USARV concluded that it should not be made standard equipment on account of its limited load capacity, and requested that all its soldiers be issued the tropical rucksack. By late 1970 the nylon field pack, with a few modifications, was in use as part of the instruction equipment, and was substituted for other uses by the larger combat pack.

These straps helped to secure the Field Pack to the suspenders when carried high on the back, without using the adapter issued with model M1956.

61

Ammunition Pouch

The LCE M1956 envisaged the M-14 to be adopted as the soldier's personal weapon, but in this new combat equipment the belt and the ammo pouches were being standardized for the various personal weapons in the US Army, such as the M-14 rifle, the M-79 grenade launcher, 12-gauge shotguns and older rifles like the Garand and the M1 carbine. The final choice was a "universal" pouch, large enough to carry ammunition for any of the different weapons.

The Pouch, Small Arms, Ammunition, Universal was a canvas pouch with a drainage eyelet at the bottom. It was closed at the top with a cover featuring a quick fastening device, similar to the one developed by the British in WWII. At the rear of the pouch were two keepers to secure it to the belt, and on the sides a system of straps for attaching two hand grenades, fastened by the spoons and secured with a press-button.

Soldiers were issued two universal ammunition pouches, one on each side of the belt buckle and, to assist in supporting the weight, one strap from the rear of the pouch attached to the ring on the front of the suspenders. In addition, the first version of the ammo pouch had a rigid inner reinforcement on the front preventing it from being crushed.

In the late 1950s, the M1956 ammo pouch could hold a bandolier of six 8-cartridge Garand clips, or eight clips inserted directly in the pouch; two 20-round BAR (Browning Automatic Rifle) magazines, or four 30-round M1 clips. In the 1960s, with the new weapons available, the pouch could carry clips for the M14 or other NATO rifles, such as the FN FAL or the H&K G3, and the pouch could easily accommodate two 20-cartridge magazines caliber 7.62 mm. Regarding the new M-16 rifle, caliber 5.56 mm, adopted in the mid-sixties, the universal ammo pouch could carry four

Detail of the metal eyelet on the first Ammunition Pouch M1956.

The interior of the pouch has no compartments.

The second Ammunition Pouch version was more flexible, as the front reinforcement was discontinued.

This model allows easy access to the M16 magazines.

A smaller pouch was manufactured especially to carry four M16 magazines

20-round magazines. It could also be used to store at least thirty cartridges for the 12-gauge shotgun or four 40 mm grenades for an M79 grenade launcher. As for hand grenades, such as the M26 fragmentation grenade, soldiers could carry two hooked to the exterior and a further three inside the pouch.

In 1962 the universal ammo pouch underwent some modifications in its design. Of these, the most notable was the removal of the front reinforcement, which made it possible to stow inside up to three M-14 magazines, instead of two as previously.

For the smaller M-16 rifle magazines, the pouch could take as many as four, but as they were shorter it was harder to extract them from the interior of the pouch. Soldiers devised homemade solutions for this problem, such as by filling the bottom of the pouch with paper or rags so that the clips would reach the edge of the opening.

In 1967, a pouch specifically designed to accommodate four M16 magazines was adopted. This was a modification on the previous model, reducing the length and removing the interior reinforcements. It was called Case, Small Arms, Ammunition, M16A1 Rifle, but did not completely replace the Universal Ammo Pouch in LCE M1956, despite the fact that by 1966 the new rifle had been distributed to all US Army units in Vietnam.

With the M1967 equipment the Case, Small Arms, Ammunition, M16 Rifle was adopted, to carry four 20-cartridge magazines, a nylon version of Case, Small Arms, Ammunition, M16A1 Rifle in M1956 equipment. As a novelty, it incorporated a new fastener with a plastic buckle that could be opened by pressing with just two fingers. This system had been designed initially for Arctic climate gear, where thick mittens are worn. To these pouches an 11-inch tape was attached on the inside, to be placed on the pouch floor before storing the magazines and, when pulled, would extract the magazines easily.

From 1965 the Army conducted trials on a bigger magazine for the M-16 rifle. Experiments were made with 30-round magazines,

The nylon version of M1967 followed the design for the smaller M16 magazine pouch. The plastic quick-release buckle could be opened even wearing thick gloves.

The ammo pouch was adapted for 30-round M16 magazines.

and were made standard issue in 1969, although their use during the Vietnam War was limited due to the problems encountered during their development. For the curved magazines, longer than the 20-round clips, a nylon bag was designed as part of the M1967 system, called Case Small Arms Ammunition (Nylon) 30 Round Magazine (M16 and M16A1 Rifle). This case had a capacity for three magazines and essentially was a longer version of

the 20-round magazine pouch. In the interior it had plastic reinforcement plates on the front and rear walls. Additionally, as a characteristic feature on many nylon items at the time, the lateral hand grenade straps had plastic press-studs.

By the mid-1960s the 30-round magazine for the M-16 was general issue and the ALICE M1972 equipment only had ammo pouches for these magazines.

First Aid/Compass Pouch

The LCE M1956 included a smaller 4 x 5 inch pouch with a lid that fastened with a press-stud. This was for carrying first aid dressings or a magnetic compass, which in previous kits were stowed in different pouches. This was called Case, First Aid Packet or Lensatic Compass M1956.

This case was attached to the equipment by a slide keeper and the position indicated in the handbook was on the belt, on the right hand side, between the buckle and the ammo pouch, or against the side of the pouch, though is was frequently seen hooked to the shoulder pad. When used as a First Aid Case, it contained a Dressing, First-Aid, Field, Camouflaged, 4 x 7 inches and a packet of Sodium Chloride-Sodium Bicarbonate for burns. When bandages were packed in more compressed sizes, two could be carried in this case.

The first version of the first aid packet only had reinforcements on the edge of the cover, and in the second model, the reinforced areas covered the edge of the entire case and a drainage eyelet was also added.

In the nylon MLCE M1967, the Case, Field First Aid Packet, Compass kept the design of the M1956 model but was made of nylon. The press-stud fastener was plastic in the first version, later replaced by metal, which was more dependable. This first aid case was not abandoned, but incorporated to the ALICE kit in 1973.

First Aid Pouch, first model.

First Aid Pouch, second model, with fully reinforced edge.

The nylon version of the First Aid/ Compass Pouch differed from the cotton model only in the reinforcements on the closure flap.

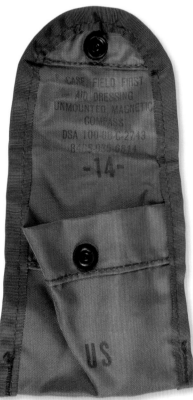

A slide keeper secures the pouch to the rest of the soldier's kit.

Metal snap on the second version of the MLCE M1967 First Aid Pouch.

Entrenching Tool and Carrier

The US Army entrenching tool at the beginning of the Cold War was the model adopted in 1945. It consisted of a spade whose blade folded over the wooden handle, with a second folding blade in the form of a pick, so that it could be used in several configurations. This combined E-tool was carried from the beginning in a V-shaped bag, with an opening at the apex for the handle to protrude. The Carrier, Entrenching Tool, M1956 is similar to the earlier M1943 on which the LTD fastener was replaced with a press-stud, and the double hook for securing it to the belt was changed for two slide keepers.

The greatest innovation on the M1956 model is that it features a special fastener to attach the bayonet scabbard, so both tools are carried together. According to the handbook, this was an alternate position for the bayonet, rather than attaching it directly to the belt, but for paratroopers equipped for a jump, it was a better option.

The entrenching tool attached to the belt on the left side, next to the butt pack, although depending on load requirements it could be hooked to the outside of any of the soldier's packs. For a jump, parachutists had to secure the spade handle to the leg with a tape, to prevent it from swinging.

A nylon carrying bag was tested, similar to the cotton M1956 issue, but the one issued in the end was quite different. The reason for this was the adoption a new aluminium spade that folded twice down to the size of the blade. The Carrier, Entrenching Tool, Collapsible, Lightweight, (Nylon) was extremely simple, without the bayonet attachment as in the previous model. The fastener was plastic, two slide keepers secured it to the belt and an interior reinforcement ran round the rim to prevent the sharp spade edges from damaging the carrier.

The Entrenching Tool could be configured in a number of positions: shown is the pick and hoe.

The Entrenching Tool Cover M1956 was similar to the earlier model, and included new slide keepers and, on the front, a bayonet hook.

Entrenching Tool showing the spade folded and unfolded.

Canteen and Cover 1 qt

In the 1950s, the US Army used a 1 qt. capacity metal canteen similar to the one adopted at the start of that century. The cover was basically the same as model M1910, manufactured in olive drab since the end of WWII, with LTD type buttons and a double hook to secure it to the belt.

After adopting LCE M1956, the Cover, Water Canteen was modified in some aspects, such as the closure with press-studs, and the fastening system to the belt, which is achieved with two slide keepers. The interior is lined with synthetic fur, as opposed to model M1910 that used thick felt. This thermal layer was useful for preserving the temperature, protection from the cold and keeping water warm in low temperature conditions; in warm climates, it provided insulation from the sun and avoided evaporation.

In 1962 the plastic 1-qt. canteen was adopted, but as its dimensions were identical to the metal version, no changes were needed in the cover issued with M1956.

Soldiers' initial kit included a cover and a 1-qt. canteen, with a metal cup. However, in Vietnam, due to the hot tropical climate, soldiers were issued two canteens and covers. They were usually worn on the belt, to either side of the butt pack, or secured to the butt pack sides.

Recce patrol members spent days on end isolated in hostile territory on their missions, during which they had to carry a large amount of equipment. To cover their water needs, these men carried extra canteens, some of which were inside their rucksack. Moreover, the covers were sometimes used as ammo pouches instead of the usual ones, as they could fit seven 20-round M16 rifle clips, that is, as many as in a seven-pocket bandolier.

Metal and Plastic Canteens, both with 1 quart capacity.

The earlier cup also adapted to the new plastic canteen.

Canteen Cover for model M1910, manufactured until the end of the 'fifties.

Earlier models to the M1956 had double hooks to secure it to the pistol belt.

The nylon canteen cover in the MLCE M1967, called Cover, Water Canteen, Nylon, 1 Quart, was similar to the M1956 model. It was made of synthetic fur lined nylon, and had plastic press-studs in the first version. An innovative development was the small pocket fastened with velcro for carrying drinking water tablets. In 1969, the plastic buttons were replaced with metal press-studs, more dependable and resistant. In 1973 the M1967 canteen cover was added to ALICE, initially called M1972 ILLCE (Individual Lightweight Load-Carrying Equipment).

The high temperatures and humidity of the tropical climate in Vietnam caused rapid dehydration of soldiers operating in the boondocks. Their water supply was vital, and it was common practice for helicop-

Canteen Cover M1956, with standard metal snaps instead of the previous "lift the dot" model.

The double hooks were replaced with slide keepers on model M1956.

ters to carry huge bladders of water to companies encamped at Remain Overnight Positions (RON). It was often the newcomers who were detailed to fill the canteens at the bladder for their squad. If no po-

table water was available, it was taken from springs or streams but always treated with tablets to prevent outbreaks of dysentery, malaria or other diseases.

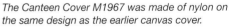

The metal snap was recovered for the Canteen Cover M1967 owing to the deficiencies of the plastic model.

The Canteen Cover M1967 was made of nylon on the same design as the earlier canvas cover.

Initially, the Canteen Cover M1967 had plastic snaps.

The Canteen Cover M1967 featured an exterior pocket for carrying water purifying tablets.

Canteen and Cover 2 qt

The 2-quart canteens were designed during WWII to meet the needs of the war in the Pacific and in Asia. Subsequently this design was not looked at again until the 1960s, with the renewed interest in Special Warfare Forces, and the growing presence of green berets in Vietnam as of 1961. As an emergency measure, the earlier 2-quart canteen was newly manufactured from nylon. This consisted of a vinyl "bladder" measuring 10 x 10 inches, with a Bakelite screw top. This bladder was inserted into a nylon case closed with a lid and a Lift the Dot closure, and had an adjustable strap for wearing across the body, or attached to the belt. More than 14 thousand of these were produced in 1962, called the Bladder and Canteen, Collapsible, 2 Quart Capacity, and the design became standard in 1963, with slight modifications.

The 2-qt Canteen was issued in Vietnam to meet soldiers' need to carry a greater water supply.

The 2-qt Canteen was flexible and adapted to the volume of water it contained, thus minimizing noise from the water in movement.

The first covers for these canteens were of rubberized cloth.

Final cover model with rectangular flap.

The first 2-qt canteen model.

After being used in south-east Asia it was found that the 2-quart Bladder Canteen was difficult to remove from the case, and the flap was re-designed so that soldiers could drink without removing the bladder from the case. This second version became standard in October 1965, and had an exterior compartment for water purifying tablets. More-over, two slide keepers were added to the back for enhanced fastening to the belt or the backpack.

Shortly after adopting the 2-quart bladder as standard, Natick Laboratories began to develop a flexible 2-qt. canteen in more rugged plastic to replace the vinyl bladder. The new Canteen, Water, Collapsible, 2 qt. Capacity was manufactured in Olive Drab colored plastic and the cap and strap were interchangeable with the 1-qt. canteen.

A cover was also designed for the 2-qt. canteen, with the same plastic fasteners as some other items in MLCE M1967, although initially it was not made of nylon but rubber

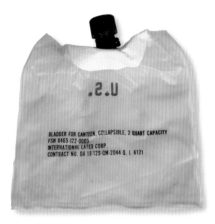  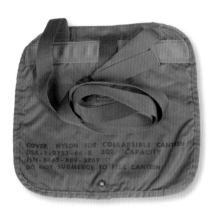

The first 2-qt Bladder model had a carrying strap.

 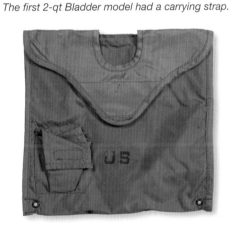 

The second 2-qt Bladder model had an opening at the top for the drinking cap, allowing the soldier to drink without removing the bladder.

The second model of the 2-qt Bladder had two slide keepers to secure it to the load carrying equipment, and a front pocket for the water purifying tablets.

coated fabric. The canteen cover, called Cover, Water Canteen, 2 qt. Collapsible, could be attached to the belt or the sides of the backpack with two slide keepers, but it also had two rings for attaching a strap, issued with the cover, and wearing it across the body. Researching and testing continued and in 1968 the cover was replaced by a nylon cover with a synthetic fur lining, similar in style to the 1-qt. canteen cover in M1967. Later on, in January 1970, another alteration was made to the cover giving it a straight flap, rather that tilted, and was standardized. This cover remained in service for several decades.

In Vietnam, distribution of the 2-qt. Bladder Canteen was limited, while the 2-qt. Collapsible Canteen was issued in large quantities and could be seen, especially among Recce troops who used to carry at least four to six quarts of water in 1- and 2-quart canteens hooked to their belt or backpack, or inside the pack or the trouser pockets.

Recce troops in Vietnam needed to carry large quantities of water and, in 1968, a higher capacity canteen was issued. The 5-qt Bladder Canteen had a vinyl interior similar to the 2-qt model but larger. The nylon outer case was designed so that it could be secured to the soldier's equipment and used as a floating aid in river crossings.

The 5-qt Bladder Canteen was designed so that it served as a floating aid, secured to the soldier's equipment.

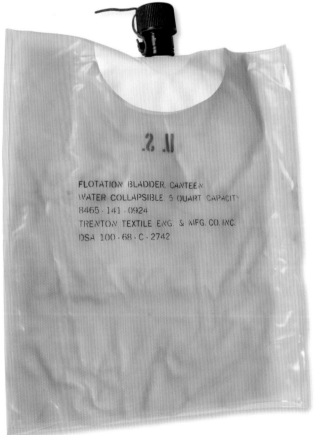

The vinyl bladder could be filled with air and used as a floating aid for 5 kg of equipment in river crossings.

Sleeping Bag Carrying Strap Assembly

Part of the soldier's essential equipment was the sleeping bag, and to carry this voluminous item the Strap, Assembly, Carrying, Sleeping Bag M1956 was devised. This was a system of straps to keep the sleeping bag rolled up and attached to the Load Carrying Equipment suspenders. It could be carried on the soldier's back, above the field pack, secured with a "quick release" fastening.

The LCE M1956 sleeping bag strap assembly was very unpopular and was often used for other purposes, especially in Vietnam, where soldiers did not carry a sleeping bag: owing to the climate conditions, this was replaced in practice by the poncho liner, used as a blanket.

For the MLCE M1967 a new, simplified model was designed: the Carrier, Sleeping Gear, consisting in a simple nylon square and two long straps to secure both the thick sleeping bag and the poncho and its liner. This assembly could be carried high on the back thanks to rings that attached to the hooks on the suspender shoulder pads. It also had a velcro fastener for carrying it secured to the belt, and a further two tapes held it steady on the suspenders to prevent it from swinging.

The Sleeping Bag Carrying Strap Assembly was also used for carrying other items of equipment when necessary.

The new model of Sleeping Bag Carrier was simpler and easier to use.

6. Parachutists´ equipment

6.1. Parachute components

The T-10 parachute consists of a series of components focused on the canopy. The canopy is stowed in the deployment bag and secured in the pack tray assembly. As the parachutist jumps from the plane, the 15-foot static line breaks the seal on the pack tray and pulls on the deployment bag freeing the suspension lines and the canopy, which are anchored to the risers attached to the jumper's harness. The parachute takes about 3 seconds to deploy and inflate, depending on the speed of the aircraft and other factors. Likewise, descent is affected by air density, wind and the supported weight.

Canopy assembly

This is the most important part of a parachute, semi-spherical in shape to capture air and slow down the fall of the attached load. A central vent at the apex allows air to escape and regulate the descent. The material must be light and highly resistant.

MC1 Canopy assembly

The MC1 Canopy assembly was manufactured in 11-ounce rip-stop nylon. The canopy was formed of 30 sections sewn together from the center to the outer edge. In turn, 30 nylon cords of 25 feet and 6 inches in length, the suspension lines, joined the canopy to the harness straps. These cords formed four groups that converged at the connector links on the straps fastened to the harness, known as risers.

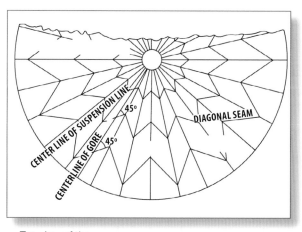

Top view of the canopy.

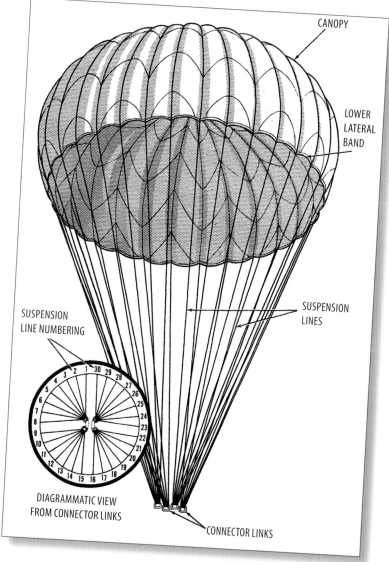

Canopy assembly

Massive drop of paratroopers in the early 1960s. The parachute used was the T-10 model.

73

The MC1 Canopy evolved over time, particularly with the addition of an anti-inversion net at the edge of the canopy to facilitate its deployment and opening. This net consisted of an 18-inch band of nylon 3 ¾ inch mesh, sewn to the skirt of the canopy and the suspension lines. Approximately 90 percent of all T-10 malfunctions were semi-inversions. Its function was to prevent the static lines from crossing over the top and dividing the canopy, causing the so-called "Mae West" effect, in an allusion to the buxom 1940s Hollywood star. The 173d Airborne Brigade used an anti-inversion net at Bong Son in December 1970.

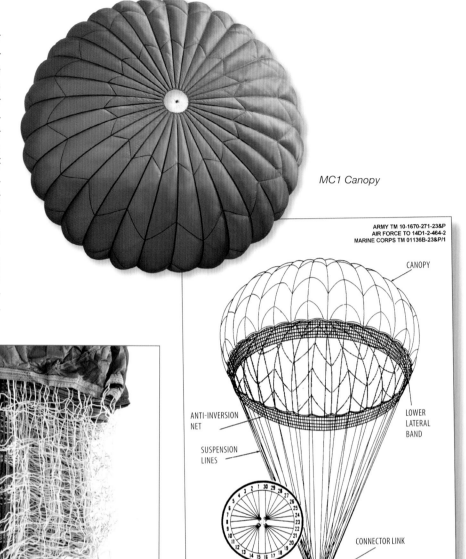

MC1 Canopy

Anti-inversion net

Canopy assembly

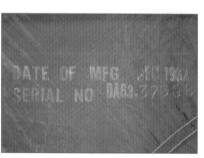

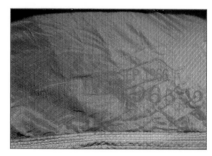
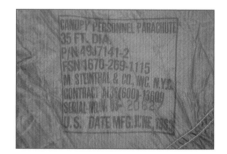

Different markings found on the canopy, depending on the manufacturer, showing the date of manufacture and canopy characteristics.

MC1 Maneuverable Canopy assembly

In 1956 the U.S. Air Force conducted a comparison test program of T-10 parachutes equipped with modifications for gliding and maneuvering; this resulted in the T-10 parachute with elliptical openings and slip risers called the Tojo parachute.

The first of the steerable parachutes was T-10 Maneuverable Parachute, which was developed by adding an oval cut (Tojo cut) in the back of the canopy with the "tuning forks" in the capewells to make the risers "slip-risers". In 1955 David Gold, a parachute development and test engineer, developed the Tojo modification. The steerable parachute and riser design were incorporated into the "Tojo" parachute, which became the mainstay parachute for the Army's special forces for a number of years. This provided more forward drive than the plain solid cloth canopy.

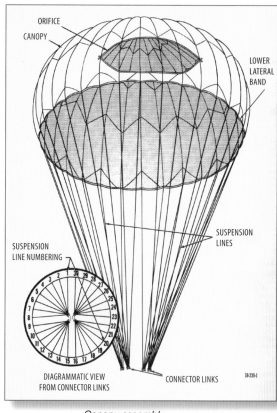

Canopy assembly.

Detail showing the Tojo cut.

The shape of this oval cut can be manipulated to maneuver the parachutist, and the oval panel cut out of the back skirt of the T-10 Maneuverable Parachute about 6 feet wide and 4 feet high that gave forward thrust to the canopy and steering control when the rear risers were pulled. Generally, steerable canopies were used by special operations forces and not in assault drops because of the possibility of accident.

The general characteristics of the MC1 maneuverable canopy were the same as those for the MC1 canopy with two exceptions, material was removed from the five gores, near the lower lateral band, to form a 39.46-square foot oval-shaped orifice at the rear of the canopy (Tojo cut) and a vent cap was added to the canopy apex reducing the apex diameter from 20 inches to 3 inches.

Vent cap detail

MC1 Maneuverable Modified Canopy assembly

The MC1 maneuverable modified canopy had an 11 gore TU modification with toggle lines, no Tojo cut and no slip risers. They did away with the slip risers because too many guys forgot to center them before landing and "Screwed into the ground". Not a good idea to land while you are still turning. The general characteristics of the MC1 maneuverable modified canopy were the same as those for the MC1 canopy with two exceptions, material had been removed from the rear eleven gores (gores 25-5), near the lower lateral band, to form a 100.4 square foot TU-shaped orifice and a vent cap was added to the canopy apex reducing the apex diameter from 20 inches to 3 inches.

MC1-1 Canopy assembly

The basic canopy is the same as that for the T-10 assembly, except that there are TU-Shaped orifices or cut-out areas, creating a horizontal velocity (a gliding type descent) like the MC1 maneuverable modified canopy. A TU modification to the canopy provides drive and maneuverability. The MC1-1 canopy is equipped with two control lines which are attached to the front side of the rear risers, each extending from an outboard orifice to toggles which may be manipulated in such a way as to make 360° turns.

The MC1-1 canopy has evolved over the years, the main improvement being an anti-inversion net which ensures excellent deployment and inflation reliability and the suspension lines that extend 18 inches below the skirt; the canopy also has two vent line centering loops (the apex centering loops). The anti-inversion net is made of 3 3/4-inch square mesh, nylon braid construction, 18-inch wide material which is attached to the inside of the lower lateral band and suspension lines to prevent inversion of the canopy. The area that the net covers between two suspension lines is called the net section.

The parachute canopy bridle loop is a length of webbing which encircles the canopy vent lines on the T-10, T-10 maneuverable, and MC1-1 parachutes. The T-10 is made of type VIII cotton webbing. The T-10 maneuverable and MC1-1 parachute canopy bridle loop is constructed from type VIII nylon webbing.

The T-10, T-10 maneuverable and MC1-1 parachutes have pocket bands attached on the outside of the canopy lower lateral band.

The canopy MC-1 of the T-10 Maneuverable Parachute and the T-10 Maneuverable Parachute Modified led to the even more sophisticated MC1-1.

Deployment Bag

This was used to store the correctly stowed canopy and the suspension lines. Attached to it is the 15-foot static line and static line snaphook attached to the free end of the static line that was hooked to the aircraft and pulled the deployment bag as the jumper exited the plane. This freed the canopy, which deployed and opened as it filled with air. The assembly was designed to function correctly in automatic mode from aircraft lateral doors and rear ramps, which were the options available in the most commonly used cargo aircraft in the US in the 1970s, such as the C-130 Hercules or the C-123 Provider. The larger of these, the C-130, could drop up to 64 parachutists in two simultaneous rows from its two side doors or the rear hatch.

With automatic opening parachutes, three types of deployment bags were used. The initial model was fitted with a locking loop closure, consisting in cotton tapes forming loops that were inserted into eyelets on the bag cover, where the bundle of suspension lines was stowed. Two versions of this bag were used: one with rows of woven loops, and another in which the cotton tape was sewn at intervals to form the rows of loops. A third model of deployment bag had a system in which the tapes that closed the mouth of the bag were joined to the tape that was released when the suspension lines pulled on the canopy during a jump. This model was only made in the version with rows of woven loops.

Deployment bag with locking loop closure and manufactured woven stow loops.

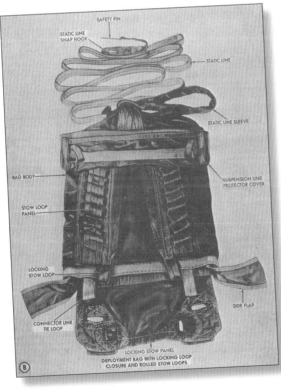

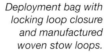

Deployment bag with locking loop closure and rolled stow loops.

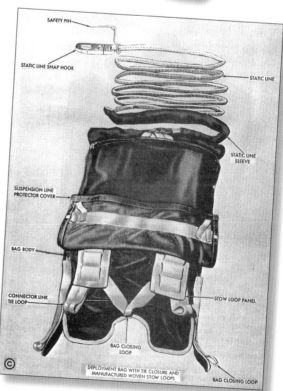

Deployment bag with tie closure and manufactured woven stow loops.

The bag was manufactured from cotton canvas, and the canopy was placed inside so that no element could damage it or prevent its extraction during a jump. On the exterior of the bag were two rows of loops into which the cord bundles formed by the suspension lines were placed, folded in an orderly fashion so that they were released without problems when the static line pulled at the bag.

The mouth of the bag was closed with a system of eyelets and loops that were opened by the tug on the suspension lines during a jump. The whole system was designed to work under any wind and speed conditions, to guarantee the jumper's safety.

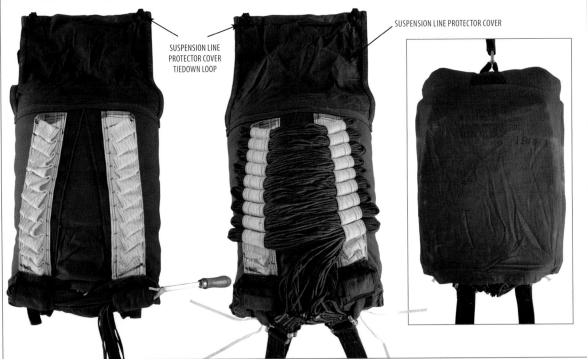

SUSPENSION LINE PROTECTOR COVER TIEDOWN LOOP

SUSPENSION LINE PROTECTOR COVER

The locking stow loop hood on the deployment bag with locking loop closure is sewn to the outside of the locking stow panel, the hoods protect locking stow loops when stow loop panel is closed and suspension lines are stowed.

Different markings found on the canopy, depending on the manufacturer, showing the date of manufacture and canopy characteristics.

The breakcord attaching strap is made of nylon webbing with one end permanently attached to the static line.

The breakcord attaching strap pocket is sewed to the inside of deployment bag body.

Breakcord tied and breakcord attaching strap stowed.

Jump from the side door of a C-119 Flying Boxcar. The static lines, with the deployment bags, remain attached to the aircraft after parachute deployment.

Snap hook with lanyard,
locked and unlocked.

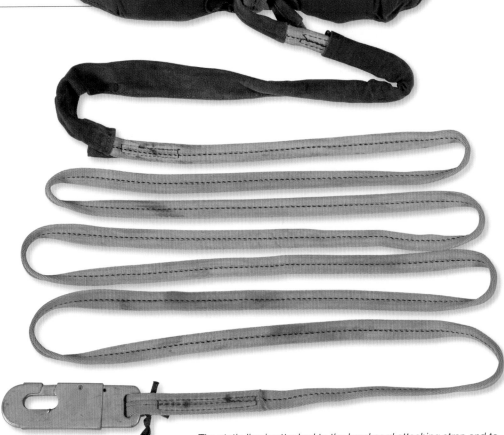

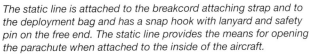

The static line is attached to the breakcord attaching strap and to the deployment bag and has a snap hook with lanyard and safety pin on the free end. The static line provides the means for opening the parachute when attached to the inside of the aircraft.

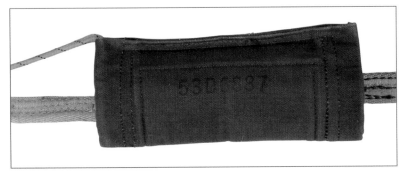

Detail of the cover protecting the static line join with the extension static line.

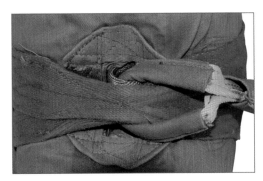

Detail of the static line attached to the breakcord attaching strap and the deployment bag.

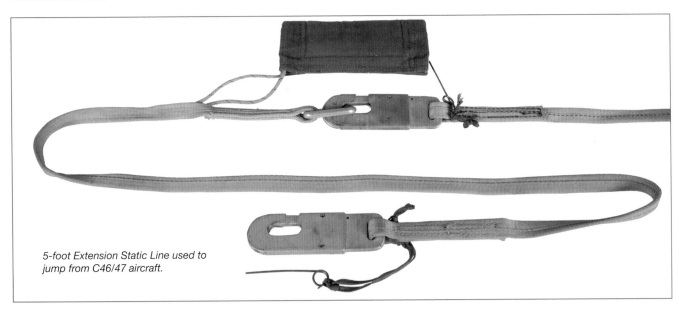

5-foot Extension Static Line used to jump from C46/47 aircraft.

Pack Tray or Parachute Pack

The pack tray was used for inclosing the deployment bag with its stowed canopy, and for stowing the static line. With a rectangular 20 x 14 in. cotton canvas or nylon floor, it had flaps on all four sides that closed and formed the pack that was attached to the jumper's harness by four back strap retainers. The four flaps on the pack tray folded together to enclose the deploy-

ment bag and were fitted with loops on the edges to form the closure system. A cotton tape, passed through the loops and knotted, withstood a weight of 160 pounds and broke under the tension on the static line in a jump.

A longer tape, with a metal buckle, came from the pack tray around the trooper's waist. This waistband,

both in the cotton and the nylon pack trays, was sewn to a central position. In a later version, the nylon waistband was sewn to the bottom of the tray to achieve a higher position of the pack on the parachutist's back. The pack tray types were a characteristic of the different models of parachute.

Pack tray of cotton material with waistband located at center of pack tray

The T-10 and MC1-1 parachutes had cotton material pack trays with a centrally placed waistband.

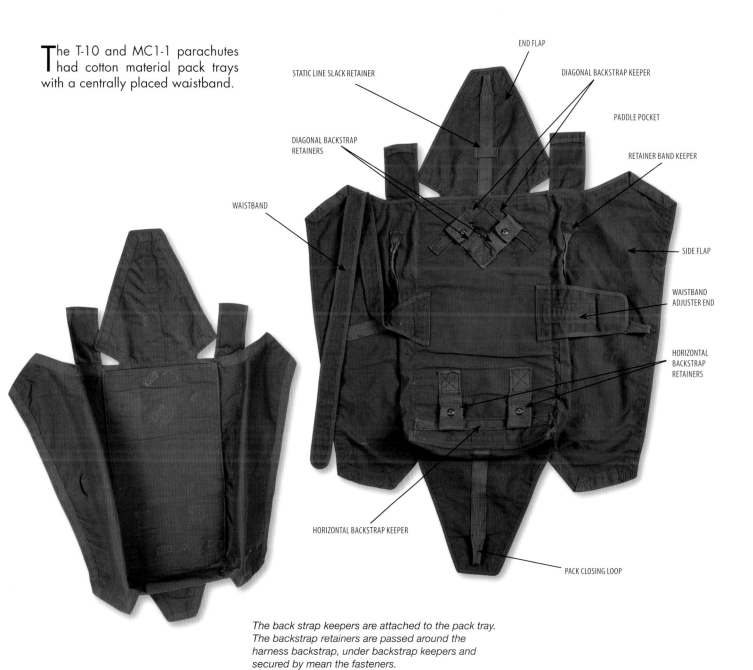

END FLAP
STATIC LINE SLACK RETAINER
DIAGONAL BACKSTRAP KEEPER
PADDLE POCKET
DIAGONAL BACKSTRAP RETAINERS
RETAINER BAND KEEPER
WAISTBAND
SIDE FLAP
WAISTBAND ADJUSTER END
HORIZONTAL BACKSTRAP RETAINERS
HORIZONTAL BACKSTRAP KEEPER
PACK CLOSING LOOP

The back strap keepers are attached to the pack tray. The backstrap retainers are passed around the harness backstrap, under backstrap keepers and secured by mean the fasteners.

The waistband is a 43-inch-long strap which may be made from two plies of webbing with binding tape stitched around the outside edges or with one ply of webbing secured inside of a top and bottom nylon duck cloth cover with binding tape sewn around the outside edges.

The waistband adjuster end has a metal adapter through which the waistband is passed to secure the pack to the user.

The retainer bands, which are made of rubber, are used on a variety of parachute packs as a means of securing static lines in position until parachute deployment is initiated. The retainer band keepers are used for attaching rubber retainer bands that hold static line stows.

The static line, hooked to a cable inside the aircraft, causes the canopy to deploy as soon as the jumper exits the plane.

Different markings found on the canopy, depending on the manufacturer, showing the date of manufacture and canopy characteristics.

Pack tray of nylon material with waistband located at center of pack tray

The T-10 and modified T-10 maneuverable parachutes had nylon pack trays with centrally placed waistband. Cotton components in the parachute pack were replaced with nylon rendering the chute reusable after immersion in salt water.

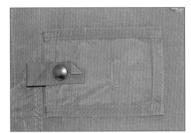

This was the only pack tray model fitted with a log record pocket.

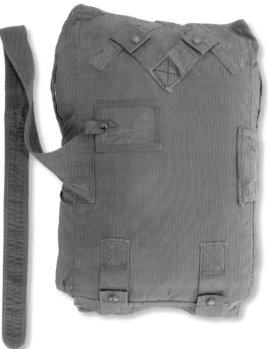

Pack tray of nylon material with waistband attached in a lower position

The T-10A and MC1-1A parachutes had nylon pack trays with the waistband in a lower position. This type of waistband, since it was adopted, also replaced the central waistbands in previous parachute models still in stock, which were altered to relocate the waistband.

Parachute risers

T-10 parachute risers

These were two 70-inch nylon web bands that joined the suspension lines to the jumper's harness, with the male fitting for the canopy release permanently fixed to the middle. This attached to the female fitting on the harness, at shoulder height, allowing the canopy to be fastened and unfastened. At the end of each riser was a connector link to which the cords of one of the four sets of suspension lines could be attached. In model T-10 the male fittings had a protective cloth cover, but this was eliminated from subsequent models as it hindered quick-release of the risers in an emergency. For jumpers attempting to release the risers to discard an unopened canopy, in order to deploy the reserve chute, it was vital to keep movements as simple as possible.

Placing the protective cover on the fitting.

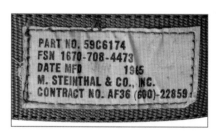

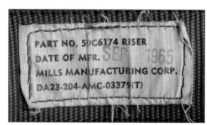

Different manufacturers' labels.

T-10 Maneuverable Parachute Risers

In maneuverable parachutes the risers were not fixed to the male fitting but could slide through it allowing the trooper to alter the inclination of the canopy and command a degree of control over his direction during descent. Each riser had a locking fork keeper into which was inserted the metal locking fork secured on each side of the harness, stopping the risers from sliding. In practice this procedure could prove difficult.

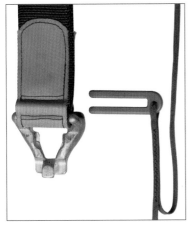 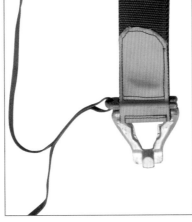

Locking fork keeper: unlocked and locked.

Pleiku, South Vietnam: Paratroopers of the 173rd Airborne Division conduct a personnel and supply parachute drop near this location during a road closing operation.

85

Maneuverable Parachute Modified Risers

Two control line bridles have been fastened to canopy radical seams 5 and 6, and 25 and 26, respectively. Two control lines have been attached by means of control line guides to the bridles, one control line to each bridle. The other ends of the control lines have been secured to the front side of the rear risers by control line guides, then run through the toggles and tied off.

Each of the 28-foot-long control lines has a reefing ring attached on the top end. The bottom end of a control line passes through a guide ting attached to the front side of a rear riser and connects to a control line toggle.

Label showing the manufacturer and the date of manufacture.

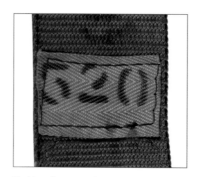

To identify stowed maneuverable parachutes a yellow label was added to the risers.

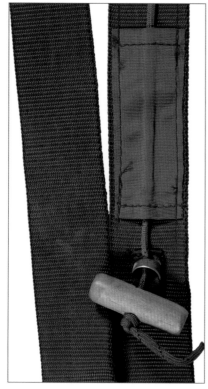

Control line guides and toggle.

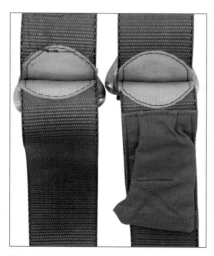

Risers on the modified T-10 Maneuverable Parachute.

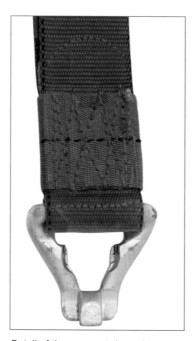

Detail of the crescent shaped stitching on the T-10 Maneuverable Parachute risers.

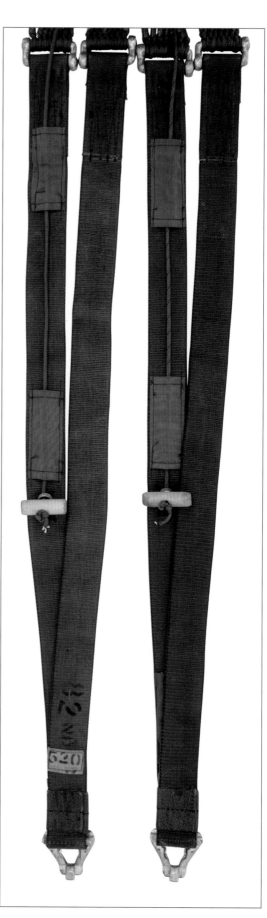

MC1-1 Parachute Risers

Other types of risers were adopted for parachute models MC1-1 and MC1-1A. These had fixed male fittings, as on the T-10, and maneuverability was achieved through control lines, 28 feet in length, reaching panels 5 and 25 on the canopy and manipulated from the risers. The rear control lines had metal and canvas guides for the control lines to pass through. A wooden toggle at the end allowed the parachutist to use the control lines to guide the descent.

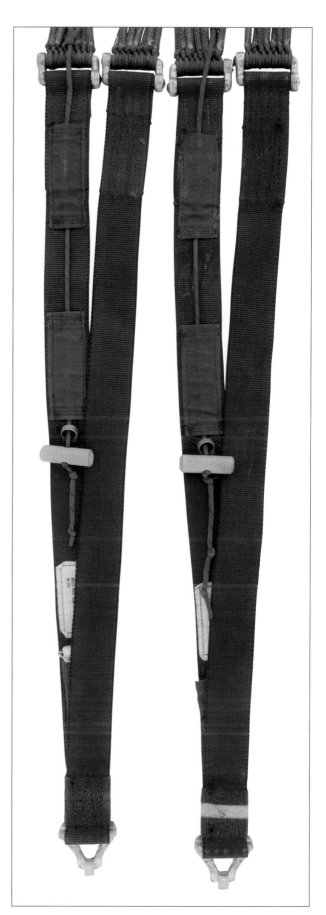

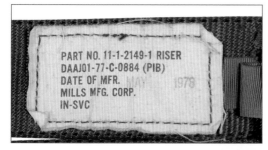

Label showing the manufacturer and the date of manufacture.

PART NO. 11-1-2149-1 RISER
DAAJ01-77-C-0884 (PIB)
DATE OF MFR. MAY 1979
MILLS MFG. CORP.
IN-SVC

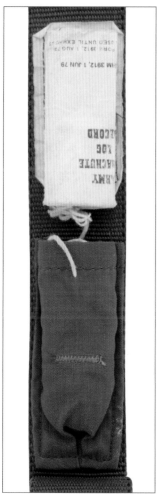

A log record pocket is installed on each riser assembly; however, only the left riser assembly pocket is used.

Control line guides and toggle.

To identify this type of risers, a yellow-ed tape was placed next to the male fittings. This was either the reinforcement tape securing the fittings, installed during the manufacture of the risers, or added later with paint or adhesive tape. This allowed the rigger to distinguish this model of parachute when packed, as it was not recognizable externally.

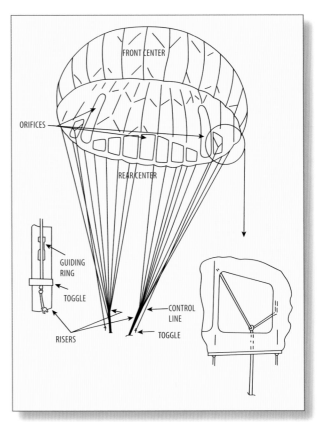

The Control Line Toggle each of the two control lines attached to the canopy has a hardwood toggle attached on the bottom end.

Canopy assembly.

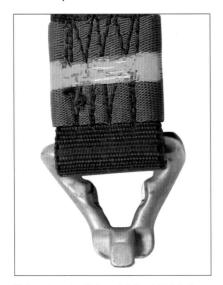

Yellow tape to distinguish the MC1-1 riser type.

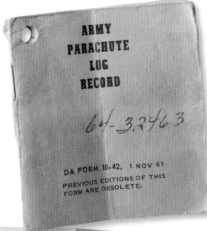

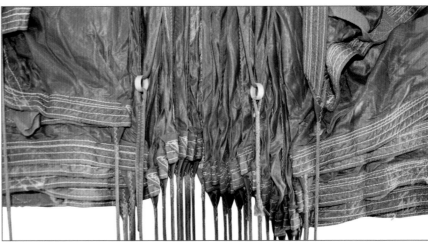

The 6-foot long Control Line Bridle is located on gores 5 and 25.

Army parachute log record, containing the parachute's characteristics and record of use.

Harness Assembly

The harness was a structure of sturdy 1 ¾ inch nylon webbing that fitted around the soldier's body. The harness was one size only as the chest, leg and back straps had metal pieces to adjust to any parachutist's body. Its function was to keep the trooper suspended from the canopy during descent.

At the shoulders were the female canopy release assemblies, to which the risers were attached with a quick-release system. This allowed the jumper to rapidly disengage the canopy in the event of landing in a strong wind or in water, and prevent being dragged. If the canopy failed to open, or only partially in-flated, the reserve parachute was activated but the main canopy was not jettisoned, and the trooper descended with both chutes. Only if the main canopy was in danger of hindering the correct deployment of the reserve chute were the risers released and the faulty canopy discarded.

Harness Assembly with Harness Quick-Release Assemblies

In the harness model featuring the quick-release assembly, the chest straps and leg straps were fitted with metal adjusting lugs connected to the harness quick release fastening system, which was a device on the center of the chest with a quick locking and unlocking mechanism.

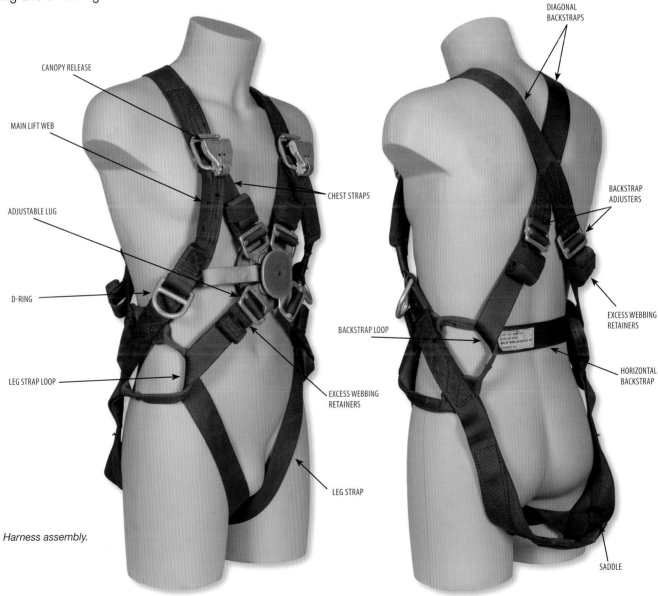

Harness assembly.

89

The main strap was of double webbing and had the chest straps and leg straps sewn to it. It ran from the canopy release assemblies to under the buttocks, where it formed a seat or 'saddle', with the leg straps. It also featured two loops forming a handle at each side of the body through which were slotted the leg straps and the diagonal back straps. On the ventral position were two D-rings to which the reserve chute was attached.

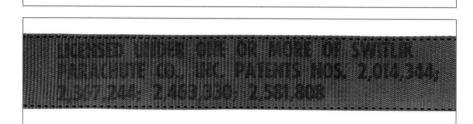
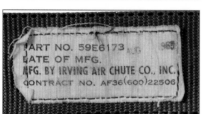

Different manufacturers' labels.

Canopy release assembly with pressure type release

During 1962, following a series of mishaps caused by wind gusts dragging paratroopers across the ground, a quick-release system was added to the assembly. This allowed soldiers a rapid means of disconnecting the main canopy upon landing.

Canopy release assembly which is constructed of aluminum secures the canopy to the parachutist by means of quick-release.

Safety clip heel in position.

Closed latch

Attaching the heel of the male fitting to the female fitting.

Safety clip closed.

Position on the harness.

A. Fit the heel of the riser male fitting into the slot of the harness female fitting.
B. Fit the toe of the riser male fitting into the groove of the harness female fitting and close the latch. Insure the latch is locked securely.
   Operate the latch and check for ease of operation.
   Close and lock the latch in position.
C. Fit the heel of the safety clip into position at the heel of the latch.
D. Close the safety clip.

Assembly of a canopy release, typical

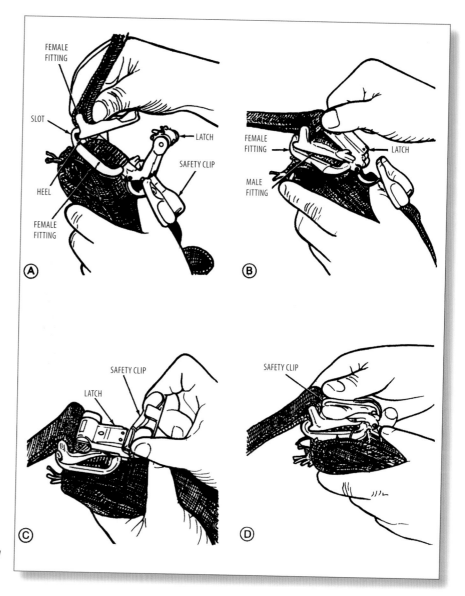

Harness Assembly with 3 Quick-Ejector Snaps

The harness model used for the T-10 parachute was replaced on MC1-1 parachutes with a new design. This new harness had a similar structure, featuring a set of nylon straps including the main strap, the chest straps, the leg straps and the diagonal back straps, but the quick-release mechanism on the previous version was eliminated.

The chest straps had quick-ejector snaps at the ends and a V-ring forming the central closure. The leg straps closed at the hips with a similar mechanism. In addition, the handle-shaped loops on the main strap were eliminated. These modifications greatly simplified the structure of the harness. The female portion of the canopy release had a cable

loop type release instead of a pressure type release. Each diagonal backstrap had six channels marked S, 1, 2, 3, 4 and L for attaching the pack tray diagonal backstrap retainer. These channels provided for six sizes ranging from small to large with four intermediate sizes. A pad was located under each quick-ejector snap and under the female portion of canopy release. There were three ejector snap pads for the ejector snaps, and two canopy release pads for the canopy release. The parachute was attached to the harness assembly securing the parachute to the paratrooper before the jump and during descent.

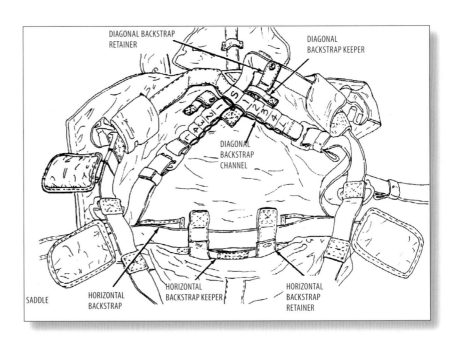

DIAGONAL BACKSTRAP RETAINER

DIAGONAL BACKSTRAP KEEPER

DIAGONAL BACKSTRAP CHANNEL

SADDLE

HORIZONTAL BACKSTRAP

HORIZONTAL BACKSTRAP KEEPER

HORIZONTAL BACKSTRAP RETAINER

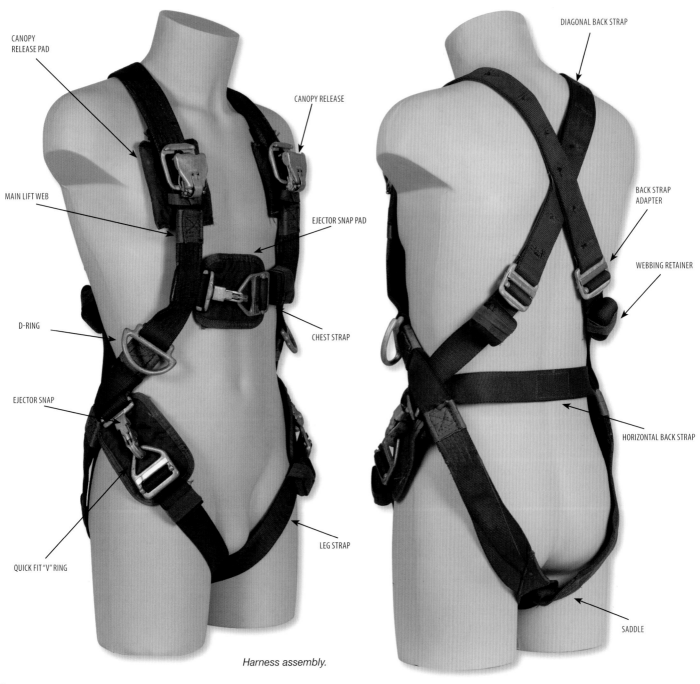

CANOPY RELEASE PAD

CANOPY RELEASE

MAIN LIFT WEB

EJECTOR SNAP PAD

D-RING

CHEST STRAP

EJECTOR SNAP

QUICK FIT "V" RING

LEG STRAP

DIAGONAL BACK STRAP

BACK STRAP ADAPTER

WEBBING RETAINER

HORIZONTAL BACK STRAP

SADDLE

Harness assembly.

The harness was designed to afford the maximum amount of maneuverability to the airborne soldier. It was fully adjustable to fit all sizes of jumper; from the 5th percentile female to the 95th percentile male. The design incorporated attachment points for a chest mounted reserve parachute and equipment rucksack.

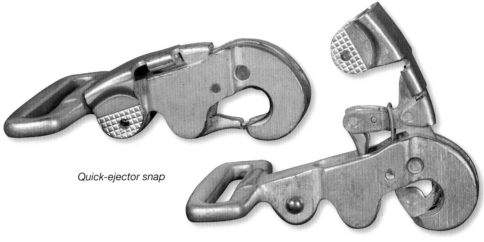

Quick-ejector snap

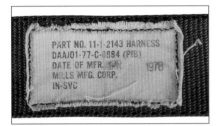

Marks and Labels

The ejector snap pad is a nylon duck, cloth covered, felt pad installed under the chest and leg strap ejector snaps on the parachute harness.

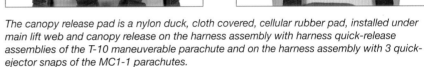

The canopy release pad is a nylon duck, cloth covered, cellular rubber pad, installed under main lift web and canopy release on the harness assembly with harness quick-release assemblies of the T-10 maneuverable parachute and on the harness assembly with 3 quick-ejector snaps of the MC1-1 parachutes.

Canopy release assembly with cable loop type release

The aluminum canopy release assembly secured the parachute to the parachutist by means of a quick-release mechanism.

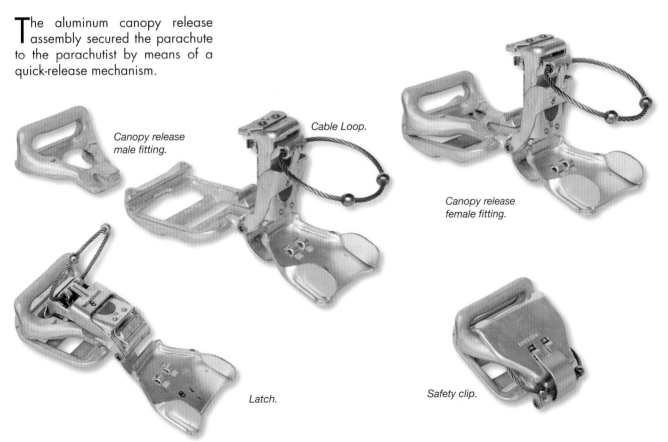

Canopy release male fitting.

Cable Loop.

Canopy release female fitting.

Latch.

Safety clip.

Attach the risers to the harness as follows:

Lay the parachute harness down with the female fittings of the harness near the male fittings of the risers.

A. Fit heel of male fitting into groove of female fitting.
B. Fit toe of male fitting into slot of female fitting, close latch and insure that the latch is secured. Operate latch and check for smooth operation.
C. Close and lock latch.
D. Position the cable loop around the latch.
E. Fit the heel of the safety clip into the slot of the latch.
F. Close the safety clip.

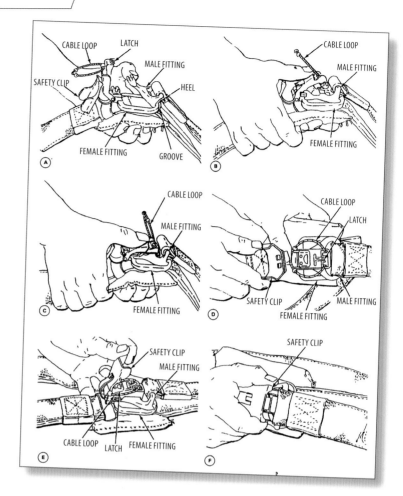

Harness Quick-Release Assembly

The central closure mechanism was an aluminum assembly allowing rapid locking and unlocking of the chest and leg straps on the parachute harness. It consisted of a round leather base and a strap with a safety pin to prevent unintentional unlocking. The mechanism was pressure-operated, so that the metal fasteners on the straps were inserted in the grooves where they remained under pressure. To free them, a wheel had to be turned and pressed. This assembly always remained fixed to the left chest strap while the other three straps were released.

The parachute harness quick release assembly used with troop-type personnel parachutes is a metal device which permits quick removal of the parachute harness from the jumper's body after the parachutist reaches the ground. This assembly consists of an aluminum alloy quick-release mechanism and a leather pad with safety clip and retainer strap.

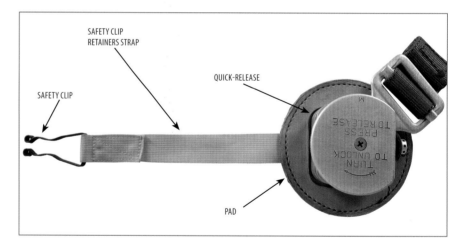

The quick release pad consists of a circular leather pad which has a retaining strap with safety clip attached.

A quick release device to free the parachutist from his canopy once on the ground had been a high priority, since the beginning of the airborne project. An early attempt at such an apparatus had been tested and rejected because it did not have a safety device to prevent it from being used while the trooper was still descending. While freeing the paratrooper from the encumbrance of his parachute was important, safety was a paramount concern. Therefore this quick-release device was rejected as unsafe, and the airborne troopers continued with the standard harness despite its drawbacks.

But by mid-1943, the tide of the war had changed, and enemy equipment became available for testing. Among the German material captured was a quick-release device used by their paratroopers. At the same time, combat experience had reinforced the imperative to develop a way to free the airborne trooper from his parachute as quickly as possible. Therefore, the German apparatus was submitted to the Test and Development Section for evaluation. Upon examining this device, the Section decided that the American-made device could work, though it would have to be modi-

fied somewhat. By the end of 1943 the modification had been made, tested, and accepted. Production was delayed while the tools needed to make the new device were produced, and then the device was delayed in reaching airborne units even further by a claim put on them by the Air Forces. However, further combat experience had strengthened the demand for the quick-release device. Eventually, by early 1945 enough of the new devices had been produced to equip the airborne units with them.

The quick-release assembly contains four spring-activated locking plungers. It has three safety features: a safety fork inserted to prevent premature release, the release operating button which must be rotated a quarter turn clockwise before it can be activated, and the requirement that the release operating button is struck before it will release.

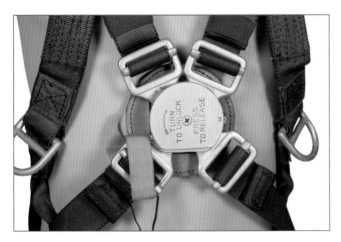

Unlocking process
Remove the safety clip from the release, rotate the operating button one quarter turn clockwise to the unlock position, depress the operating button with the palm of one hand, and remove the three harness lugs from the locking plungers. The quick release was preferred if the trooper was liable to drift into a body of water.

Locking process
Insert the right chest strap into the quick-release assembly and place the safety clip behind the outer disk of the quick-release assembly. Pass the leg straps through the leg strap loops from inside to outside, making a quarter turn toward the body, and insert the adjustable lugs into the quick-release assembly until a click is heard.

6.2. Parachute models

The T-10 parachute was adopted for mass airborne jumps and for paratrooper training purposes. For an aircraft at a speed of 104 mph (90 knots), the minimum drop altitude was 1250 feet for Airborne training jumps, 1000 feet for Tactical training jumps, 900 feet for Wartime training jumps and the altitude established in the tactical orders for drops in combat operations.

The T-10 evolved through a succession of improvements, in particular toward models with a certain capacity for maneuvering during descent. Further, during the transition periods it was common practice to set up parachutes combining different elements, as the deteriorated elements were replaced with parts from the updated models.

T-10 Main Troop-Back Parachute

35-foot diameter T-10 troop back parachute assembly

The T-10 parachute was standardized by the US Government to equip parachute troops from the early 1950s and was called T-10 Non-Maneuverable Main Troop-Back Parachute. This chute had an MC-1 canopy, 35 feet in diameter, featuring static line automatic opening, and the canopy was stowed in a deployment bag that, in turn, was stowed inside the pack tray assembly. It could carry a trooper safely from an aircraft with full combat load in vertical drops over the enemy. It was used by the US Army for mass drops of troops both in combat and training situations. In the fifties, one of the most commonly used aircraft was the C-119 *Flying Boxcar*, from which jumpers exited the side doors, while the rear

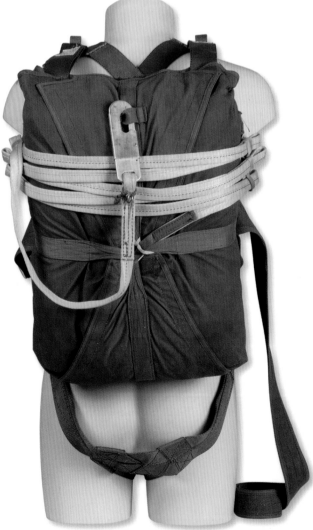

hatch was used only for dropping supplies, for which it took off without the large tail section doors.

The complete T-10 parachute weighed 29 pounds and could be used to jump from a plane traveling at up to 173 mph at a minimum altitude of 500 feet, with maximum permissible wind conditions of 15 mph. It withstood a maximum weight of 360 pounds, and the rate of descent was between 22 and 25 feet per second. Its service life was 12 years, and had to be repacked every 120 days. Riggers were responsible for ensuring the parachutes were correctly packed; they were sealed and stored until required for a jump.

Main components of the T-10
Canopy, 35 feet in diameter without anti-inversion net.
A cotton canvas deployment bag, either with rolled stow loops or with manufactured woven stow loops.
A cotton canvas pack tray or parachute pack with a central waistband.
Two-riser assembly with canopy release covers.
Harness assembly with pressure type canopy release.
Harness quick-release assembly.

In 1975 it was modified to the T-10A, which had a harness with snap hooks and D-rings instead of the quick-release assembly. A year later, the T-10B incorporated an anti-inversion mesh on the canopy, as its main innovation. In 1986 the T-10C was adopted, modifying certain features on the canopy, which in practice meant greater skirt diameter and a slower rate of descent.

35-foot diameter T-10 maneuverable troop back parachute assembly

The T-10 Maneuverable Parachute was a first attempt at gaining control over the direction of descent. It incorporated certain characteristics of both the T-10 parachute and the HALO (free-fall) parachute. This parachute model had an MC1 Maneuverable Canopy, with an oval shaped vent that affected five panels at the rear of the canopy, and a hood at the apex to maintain a rate of descent of 15 to 22 feet per second. In addition, the risers could be manipulated to vary the canopy inclination, and the pack tray was constructed in nylon canvas with a central waistband. The remaining parachute elements were those of model T-10.

This maneuverable parachute was developed to meet a requirement stated in 1961 by the U. S. Army Special Warfare School. The parachute was tested by the U. S. Army Airborne, Electronics and Special Warfare Board at Fort Bragg in 1962 and soon become standard piece of equipment for Special Forces and some specialized units.

Controlling the canopy during descent is different from controlling the standard T-10 parachute. In theory, pulling the risers and orienting the canopy vent towards or away from the wind would cause the parachute to gain or lose speed. Should the opening be placed at an angle to the wind, lateral movement would occur.

In this parachute, the manual slip risers have locking forks which can be used when jumping from altitudes over 1500 feet actual. By removing them, more positive slips can be made.

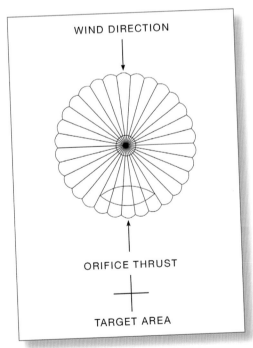

When the orifice is located in a direction away from the wind, the thrust of the orifice will be acting directly against the wind. This reduces the effect of wind velocity on the canopy and will retard the movement of the canopy in the direction of the wind.

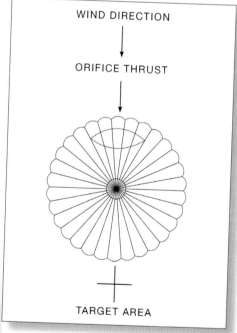

When the orifice is located into the wind, the thrust of the orifice combines with the thrust of the wind to speed the movement of the canopy in the direction of the wind.

This type of parachute could not be used at speeds under 58 mph, and given its capacity to change direction during the descent it was mandatory for the jumper to look on all sides before maneuvering with the risers to avoid collision with other jumpers.

The maneuverable parachute, by letting air escape through the orifice in the canopy, also gives the jumper a horizontal push to the front. If the wind is at your back, both horizontal pushes combine, causing the jumper to pick up quite a bit of horizontal speed. This usual-

ly results in a "crash and bum" type Parachute Landing Fall, with the accompanying aches, pains, and broken bones – or worse. If the wind is at your front, however, the horizontal pushes tend to counteract each other, letting the jumper down nice and easy.

After checking the canopy, the parachutist will determine the location of nearby jumpers and then remove the slip riser locking forks. The slip risers may then be used to maneuver the parachute toward a specific target.

35-foot diameter T-10 maneuverable modified troop back parachute assembly

With the T-10 Maneuverable Parachute Modified a greater capability for control during descent was achieved. This parachute had the capability to consistently put personnel into a small area and this accuracy could be highly advantageous for paracommando work, because It could put a small combat force, such as a special forces team, into a 50-meter square. This was not possible with the standard T-10 and extremely difficult with a maneuverable T-10.

It had an MC1 Maneuverable Modified Canopy, with an opening across 11 panels in a T-U configuration. This allowed a speed of between 16 and 23 feet per second to be maintained, and its use was limited to aircraft traveling at speeds of between 50 and 130 mph.

The T-10 Maneuverable Parachute Modified had about two-and-a-half times more forward speed than the standard MC-1 canopy. That meant that a jumper could stand up to an 18-knot crosswind and still come down with his head pointing skyward, or make a long run over a drop zone to reach a distant target.

Another advantage was the chute's quick opening time which allowed drops from lower altitudes and, hence, more accuracy.

Further to the canopy, it differed from the earlier T-10 Maneuverable Parachute in its fixed risers, with no sliding action, featuring instead control lines to alter the inclination of the canopy. As in the preceding model, the direction of movement depended on the wind speed and the orientation of the canopy vent. Its maneuverability required that jumpers kept a separation of 50 feet during descent.

35-foot diameter T-10A troop back parachute assembly

The T-10A Parachute appeared in 1975 with some changes with respect to the T-10, but had the same canopy and risers, and therefore the same capabilities and limitations, although its rate of descent was between 19 and 23 feet per second. The T-10A model also had an improved harness, replacing the quick-release assembly with quick ejector snap hooks and D-rings on the chest and leg straps. Furthermore, the female canopy release devices had a cable loop type release instead of the previous model's pressure release. The remainder of components coincided with the T-10 with the exception of the pack tray, made of nylon canvas with a low-set waistband.

35-foot diameter T-10B troop back parachute assembly

The T-10B Parachute was adopted in 1976 and had the same characteristics as its predecessor, the T-10A, except for its weight, which increased to 31 pounds.

The innovation was in the canopy, which now had an anti-inversion net. The remainder of components were those of the T-10A.

MC1-1 main troop-back parachute

35-foot diameter MC1-1 troop back parachute assembly

The MC1-1 was introduced in the early 1970s for the same purposes as the T-10 but with superior maneuverability. Its name, MC, stands for "Maneuverable Canopy". This parachute made it possible to plan airborne jumps with great precision over small drop zones. It featured the T-10 canopy modified with TU vents and two control lines manipulated from the risers that varied the inclination of the canopy. Thanks to these elements the parachute acquired horizontal drive and the capacity for 360-degree turns. The pack tray was constructed in nylon canvas with the waistband in the center, and the harness had a quick-release assembly with pressure-type female canopy release devices.

Parachutist with a MC1-1 model chute.

35-foot diameter MC1-1A troop back parachute assembly

This chute appeared in 1975 and differed from the previous version in the replacement of the harness with quick-release assembly by the new model with quick ejector snap hooks and D-rings on the chest and leg straps. This harness, which also featured the female canopy release devices from the cable loop type release model, replaced the harness on the MC1-1 model and, as worn components on older models were substituted, they were re-named as MC1-1A. The nylon pack tray with the waistband in the low-set position was also fitted on model MC1-1 as worn components were replaced.

35-foot diameter MC1-1B troop back parachute assembly

In 1976 the MC1-1B parachute arrived as an improved version of model MC1-1A, incorporating an 18-inch mesh anti-inversion net on the canopy skirt.

The components on this parachute were identical to those on the previous model except for the risers, which were shortened to 30 inches.

Paratrooper of the 82nd airborne Division jumps from a UH-1 'Huey' helicopter in the late seventies.

T-10 Reserve Parachute

This was a non-maneuverable parachute carried on the chest and deployed manually. It was used as a reserve chute, activated by the jumper in the event of malfunction of the dorsal T-10. The complete pack weighed 12 pounds and had the same requirements regarding use as the T-10 backpack parachute.

The T-10 reserve parachute consisted of a pilot chute, a canopy assembly, a pack assembly and a ripcord.

When the locking pins are withdrawn from the cones, the side and end flaps of the pack spring apart and the spring activated pilot chute is ejected.

Different manufacturers' labels.

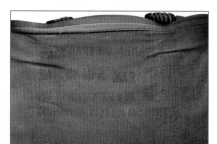

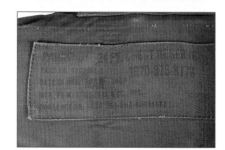

A commercial praising paratroopers' virtues.

Markings differed depending on the manufacturer.

Paratrooper equipped with a T-10 Reserve Parachute attached to the parachute harness assembly. A folded kit bag is secured at chest height behind the reserve parachute for use after landing.

Pilot chute

The pilot chute extracted the canopy so that as soon as the pack assembly was deployed, a spring launched the pilot chute, which acted as an air anchor pulling and deploying the canopy. Octagonal in shape, 3 feet and 4 inches in diameter, it opened like an umbrella with a spring action.

The reserve parachute was deployed when the main chute failed and the jumper's rate of descent was too high.

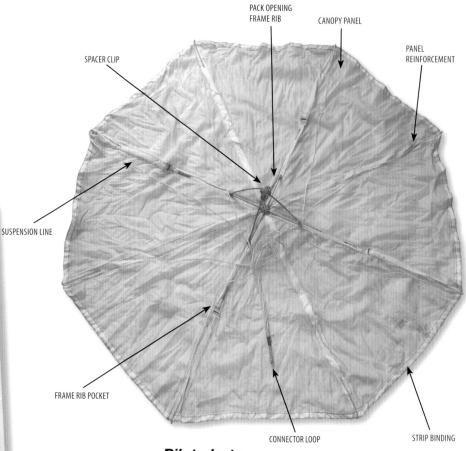

PACK OPENING FRAME RIB — CANOPY PANEL — PANEL REINFORCEMENT — SPACER CLIP — SUSPENSION LINE — FRAME RIB POCKET — CONNECTOR LOOP — STRIP BINDING

Pilot chute

Canopy assembly

The canopy was a 24-inch diameter circle of nylon fabric, constructed in 24 panels and 24 suspension lines each 20 feet long. It formed a central apex with a bridle line attaching it to the pilot chute. Owing to its smaller size, descending with this canopy only was a greater risk, and whenever possible troopers used this chute at the same time as the damaged canopy, to reduce the rate of descent.

Canopy assembly.

Initially the canopy was white, but this was modified to green.

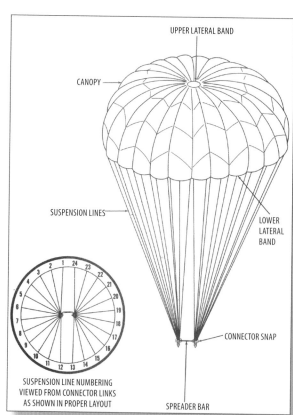

UPPER LATERAL BAND — CANOPY — SUSPENSION LINES — LOWER LATERAL BAND — CONNECTOR SNAP — SPREADER BAR

SUSPENSION LINE NUMBERING VIEWED FROM CONNECTOR LINKS AS SHOWN IN PROPER LAYOUT

Pack assembly

The pack assembly was rectangular and four side panels closed together to house the canopy and the suspension lines properly stowed in the interior. The panels were secured by a system of pins and metal eyelets blocked with the ripcord. When this closure was freed, the pack assembly flaps opened thanks to three spring bands on the exterior of the pack. In addition, the pack had one or two carrying handles and two openings on the bottom through which the riser quick-ejector snap hooks passed, and to which the canopy suspension lines were attached.

Pack assembly interior.

Ripcord

The reserve parachute was activated when the ripcord was pulled manually. This was a ring on a steel wire with two pins locking the pack assembly closure. Pulling on the ring freed the closure and the canopy deployed thanks to a system of springs and the wind pulling the pilot chute.

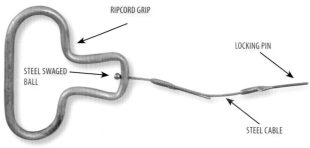

RIPCORD GRIP

STEEL SWAGED BALL

LOCKING PIN

STEEL CABLE

Position of the reserve parachute.

6.3. Combat Loads

Five Special Forces paratroopers. Left to right: **Infantryman** equipped with Rucksack and H_Harness, **HALO** (High Altitude, Low Opening) and **HAHO** (High Altitude, High Opening), **Mountaineer**, **Frogman** and **Paratrooper** equipped with parachutist rough terrain system.

Parachutists had to jump carrying all the necessary gear to perform their assigned tasks after landing. Jumps were either with individual loads, weapons, and collective equipment, but these loads had to be as light as possible and appropriate for the mission. Soldiers only jumped carrying the essential equipment to ensure their capability for immediate combat readiness.

Any further materiel would be deployed by other airborne means.

Wearing of Combat Equipment

Wearing of unit Combat Equipment

Radios and other equipment such as telephones, wire, wire reels, additional small arms ammunition and mines, may accompany the individual load-carrying equipment provided the total load does not exceed 35 pounds. Loads in excess of 35 pounds should be carried in the parachutist's adjustable equipment bag or weapon and individual equipment container.

Wearing of Individual Combat Equipment

For safety reasons, troopers put on their gear in such a way as to prevent injury or hampering their parachute. Hard or voluminous items needed to be kept away from the thighs or buttocks, and to avoid metal and wooden items from coming into contact they were carried separated by buffer material. Likewise, all snaps, hooks and other sharp items were covered in adhesive tape to prevent them from snagging.

Steel Helmet

Paratroopers used the M1-C helmet, which differed from the M1 infantry helmet in an additional fastening system to prevent the helmet from falling off as the trooper exited the aircraft.

The union between the liner and the shell was reinforced with metal press-studs at the end of the chinstrap and on the interior of the liner.

The liner in the M1-C helmet had inverted-A shaped straps on each side, with a buckle at the apex to fasten the parachutist's chinstrap. This consisted of a canvas tape with an extra piece sewn in the center and fitting over the chin, while the main strap passed under the chin. In addition, to fasten the chinstrap to the helmet shell, it had to be inserted through the horizontal piece of the inverted-A on the liner. The objective was to ensure the helmet fitted as securely as possible and to prevent it from falling off or tilting and injuring the jumper.

During the parachute drop in Operation Junction City paratroopers wore a colored tape on their helmets as a marker to help the various companies to regroup after landing.

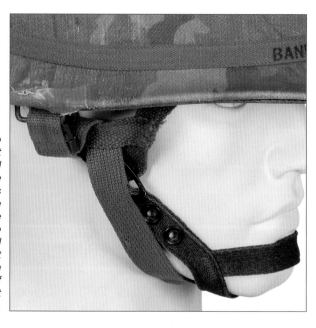

Interlace the chinstrap of the steel helmet through the horizontal piece of webbing on the side of the parachutist's chinstrap and secure it under the chin. The parachutist's chinstrap is worn with the sewed portion across the front of the chin, and with the continuous piece of webbing under the point of the chin.

Individual Equipment Belt "Pistol Belt"

The Individual Equipment Belt, or Pistol Belt, was worn under the parachute harness, in the normal fashion on the soldier's waist but unbuckled, in order to leave the belly area free.

Combat Field Pack Suspenders

The Combat Field Pack Suspenders were worn under the parachute harness fastened to the pistol belt at the front and rear hooks, instead of connecting these to the eyelets on the Butt Pack. In this way, the Butt Pack sits a little lower and does not interfere with the Pack Tray Assembly.

Universal Small Arms Ammunition Pouch

The two Universal Small Arms Ammunition Pouches issued to soldiers were fastened on either side of the pistol belt buckle, as far to the sides as possible. The ammo pouch straps, normally fastened to the metal loops on the suspenders, were attached to each other at the waist front. As soon as the trooper released his chute, he fastened his pistol belt and the ammo pouch straps were returned to their normal position.

Spc. 4th Bill O'Connell of the 101st Airborne Division, wearing the LCE M1956 under his T-10 parachute, in June 1963.

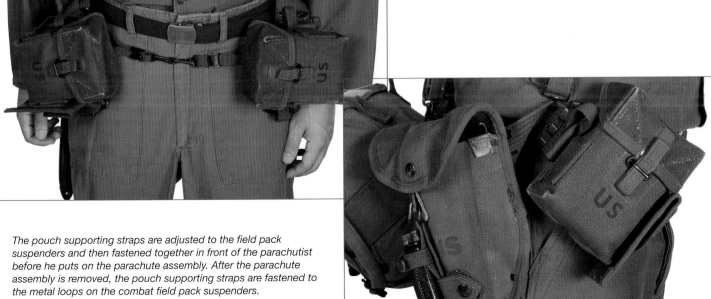

The pouch supporting straps are adjusted to the field pack suspenders and then fastened together in front of the parachutist before he puts on the parachute assembly. After the parachute assembly is removed, the pouch supporting straps are fastened to the metal loops on the combat field pack suspenders.

Combat Field Pack "Butt Pack"

At the back of the pistol belt was the Combat Field Pack, or Butt Pack, secured with two metal fasteners, but not attached to the suspenders. These straps had to be well stowed to avoid snagging, and adhesive tape was used to keep them out of the way.

Inside the butt pack was the poncho, a MX-991/U Flashlight and one of the three daily meals issued as combat rations. However, if the trooper carried a larger rucksack he generally did not use the field pack.

First Aid/Compass Pouch

The First Aid/Compass Pouch was carried as per regulations, fastened either to the left side of the right ammo pouch, or to the pistol belt, in front of said ammo pouch. It was forbidden to wear it in the other normal position, namely high up on the suspenders, as it would interfere when donning the parachute assembly harness.

Canteen with Cup and Cover

The Canteen with Cup and Cover was carried on the left of the pistol belt in a position below the soldier's armpit, so that when taking up his weapon the canteen remained between the weapon and the sling.

Entrenching Tool with Carrier and Bayonet with Scabbard

The Entrenching Tool was carried in its holder, fastened to the pistol belt on the right, so that it was below the parachute harness and slightly toward the back of the trooper's leg. The tool handle was tied securely to the thigh with cotton cord or tape.

The Bayonet and Scabbard were carried as per regulations on the eyelets and straps expressly fitted to the Entrenching Tool Carrier for this purpose.

MC-1 Parachutist´s Knife

The lanyard on the Parachutist´s Knife or MC-1 Survival Knife was tied to the buttonhole on the left border of the jacket, and when donning the parachute it was allowed to hang inside the trooper´s clothing.

In 1958, the Air Force adopted a knife called the "MC-1 Survival Knife." The most noticeable thing about this new jump knife was the bright orange plastic handle scales. The other significant change from the MC-1 was that a manually opened blade was added in addition to the automatic blade. This is universally called "Shroud line cutter."

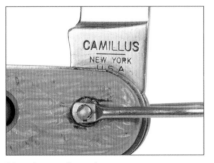

Manufacturer's mark.

Ammunition and Hand Grenades

Ammunition for the personal weapon was carried in two ammo pouches, and additional magazines in the ammo bandoliers or the trouser pockets.

Hand grenades were carried inside their containers in the interior of the parachute kit bag or the rucksack.

M17 Protective Field Mask

The M17 Protective Field Mask and its accessories were stowed inside their carrier, which was secured to the right leg with two straps. The mouth of the carrier was placed facing forward next to the leg.

Individual equipment

Weapons

Individual weapons had to be carried in the M1950 Adjustable Individual Weapons Case whenever available, but the operation commander could decide whether these weapons were to be carried directly on the trooper's body in any specific manner or field expedient method. This entailed certain risks that the commander had to take into consideration, and particular care had to be taken inside aircraft during operation immediately before a jump, both regarding the static line and the interval between jumpers.

One of the main hazards when applying a field expedient method is that the weapon may injure the soldier on landing. Another is that, should the muzzle be pointing downward, it may become entangled with the parachute suspension lines or those of another jumper if a collision occurs. Should the muzzle be pointing upward, however, it may become entangled in the static line on exiting the aircraft. To prevent these hazards, on USAF aircraft weapons must be carried on the left shoulder with the muzzle pointing down. These regulations may vary at different times, and during the drop in Operation Junction City, paratroopers carried their M-16 rifles with the muzzle pointing upward, despite being aboard USAF aircraft.

M14 Rifle

Preparing the M14 rifle for a jump consists in shifting the sling to a higher position, fitting it tightly around the stock and barrel. This prevents the barrel from protruding when the weapon is slung on the shoulder. It is also protected with adhesive tape on the buttstock plate, metal parts on the sling and the sights.

Soldiers hold the M14 against their left side so that the barrel protrudes as little as possible and with the operation rod toward the outside. The sling was passed in front of the D-ring on the parachute harness, becoming immobilized on donning the reserve parachute.

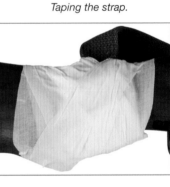
Taping the strap.

Taped buttstock.

Position of the sling.

Sling position on the sight.

Taped sight.

To ensure the weapon remains close to the trooper's body, the pack tray waistband is passed over the rifle and, additionally, with the aid of cotton tapes, the stock is firmly secured to the leg and the sling to the harness strap.

On all individual weapons the tape securing them to the trooper's leg must be removed before landing to allow freedom of movement and to avoid injury.

M16 and M16A1 Rifle

To don the M16 assault rifle for a jump, the sling had to be extended to its maximum length and adhesive tape placed on the metal keeper. The operating handle and the mounted bolt assist were also protected with adhesive tape. Likewise, the magazine was secured with adhesive tape to safeguard against losing it accidentally, and the muzzle was covered to prevent it from getting tangled in the suspension lines –as the early models of M16 with a three-pronged flash hider were liable to do – or dirt from entering on landing.

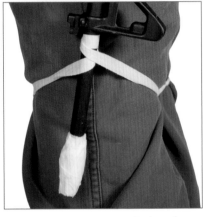

The lower tiedown secures the barrel (muzzle down) or butt (muzzle up) of the rifle to the parachutist's leg to prevent possible entanglement with the suspension lines of the parachute. It is removed prior to landing to avoid injury to the parachutist.

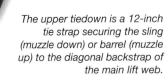

The upper tiedown is a 12-inch tie strap securing the sling (muzzle down) or barrel (muzzle up) to the diagonal backstrap of the main lift web.

More painstaking preparations also included securing with adhesive tape the ejector port cover to prevent dust getting inside, and the handguard to ensure it did not break off on impact with the ground.

The weapon was carried on the left shoulder with the sling pinned down by the reserve chute, and with the waistband over it.

When the M16 was carried with the muzzle upward, the buttstock was tied to the leg with cotton tape and the barrel to the main strap on the parachute harness. On board USAF aircraft the weapon was required to be carried muzzle down, the pistol grip toward the rear and the tapes securing the barrel to the leg and the sling to the main strap on the harness.

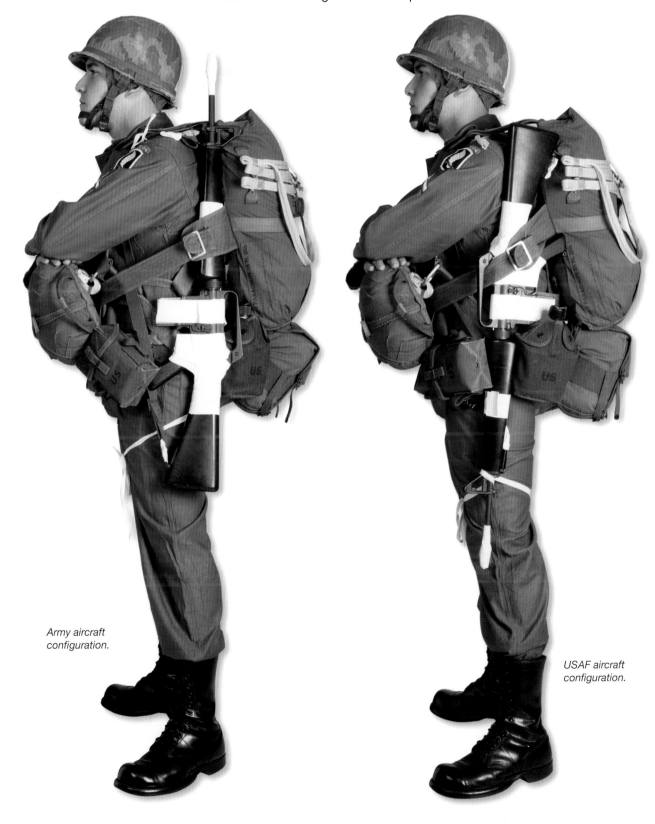

Army aircraft configuration.

USAF aircraft configuration.

M79 Grenade Launcher

Soldiers armed with an M79 grenade launcher had to extend the sling to three quarters of its length and apply adhesive tape to the metal keeper. Tape was also used to protect the muzzle, to keep out dirt, and to cover the sight; the leaf-type sight, which being large and having folding action could easily get caught on objects; the sling swivel, liable to get caught on the suspension lines; and the breech lock, which could open the gun and cause an obstruction.

The M79 was hung from the left shoulder with the trigger guard facing forward. The sling was pressed in place with the reserve parachute and the waistband passed over the weapon. Additionally, the buttstock was tied with cotton tapes to the leg and the sling to the main strap on the parachute harness.

The upper tiedown secures the sling to the main lift web and the lower tiedown secures the butt to the jumper's leg to prevent possible entanglement with the parachute suspension lines. The lower tiedown is removed prior to landing to avoid injury to the jumper.

M60 Machine Gun

When the M60 Machine Gun and its accessories were transported by a single soldier, it was carried in a Parachutist's Adjustable Equipment Bag or in a Weapon and Individual Equipment Container. If it was shared between two soldiers, one carried the weapon in an Individual Weapon Case, while the other took charge of the complementary items using an Individual Weapon Case and a Kit Bag.

Pistol

The pistol was carried in its leather holster attached on the right side of the pistol belt, securing the holster with a lanyard and preventing the flap from opening with a piece of adhesive tape.

Other weapons

Weapons not mentioned here could be jumped in a similar manner. The left shoulder was used for slinging weapons. An upper tiedown kept the weapon on the shoulder and a lower tiedown prevented the weapon from rotating toward the jumper's face during parachute deployment. The weapon should not restrict the points of contact and should have sharp or irregular edges taped or padded to prevent injury. The muzzle should also be protected if there is a possibility of its becoming clogged with dirt or mud upon landing. The weapon should also be rigged so there is no interference between the static line or other parts of the parachute during deployment. Usually the sling had to be resecured (use of half hitch instead of sling keeper) to prevent loss from the opening shock during canopy inflation.

H Harness

This consisted of two nylon 56-inch straps joined by a further two straps 11 inches long. Each of the long straps had two friction adapters at one end, one for closing the straps and the other, with a quick-release mechanism, to attach an additional 18-inch strap ended in a snap hook.

The H-harness was designed to secure the Kit Bag or the Rucksack and hook them to the D-rings on the parachute harness.

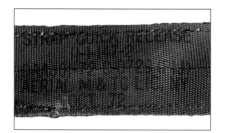

Manufacturer's label.

Aviator's Kit Bag

The Kit Bag, made of cotton canvas, had two handles, a zip closure and metal snaps on the top. It was used to stow the parachute after landing or to carry personal equipment or other additional items.

The Kit Bag is secured by a zipper and snaps which extend across the top of the bag.

Markings differed according to the manufacturer.

EASTERN CANVAS PRODUCTS, INC
NOVEMBER 1963
8460-606-8366

When empty, the Kit Bag was carried folded flat against the body under the quick-release assembly. The handles were placed facing upward and the right chest strap was slotted through them.

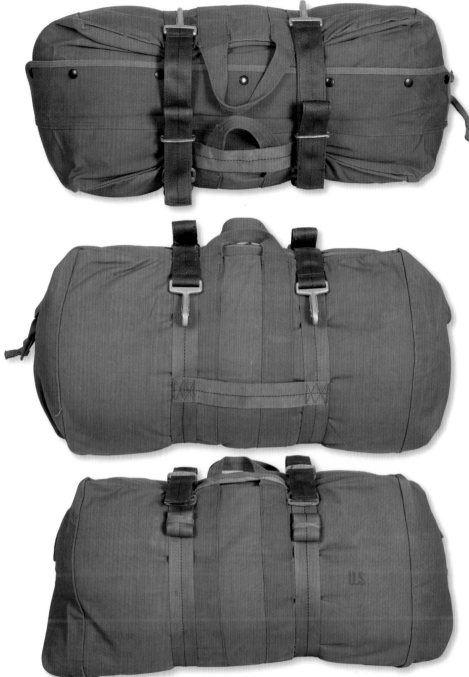

Paratroopers wearing individual combat equipment carried the Kit Bag folded flat against the body, or used it to load their combat equipment.

When stowing equipment in the Kit Bag, care had to be taken to ensure the contents could be extracted easily and ready for use. After closing the bag, it was placed centered on the H-harness and surrounded by the straps, which were then tightened to hold it firmly in place. The straps fitted with snap hooks, regulated to a length of 6 to 8 inches, slotted through the bag handles and fastened to the D-rings on the parachute harness.

After landing, the soldier had to release the snap hooks from the friction adapter, thanks to the quick-release system, and remove the Kit Bag. Then he had to release the snap hooks from the D-rings and replace them on the H-harness.

Detail of the quick-release system.

In an emergency, the Kit Bag could be released before landing using the same method thanks to the quick-release on the friction adapter.

Rucksack

Its use became generalized in the US Army during the 1960s. Constructed in nylon canvas, it consisted of a main compartment and three exterior load pockets, built on an aluminum frame with straps for securing additional loads.

The contents had to be protected from accidental impacts and it was therefore recommended to stow soft items near the front, which was the area liable to come into contact with other equipment.

The rucksack was carried inverted, with the base of the frame at the top, fastened to the H-harness and hooked to the D-rings on the parachute harness.

Rucksack inverted for a jump.

Place the H-harness on the rucksack so that the cross straps are in front of the rucksack and the friction adapters are touching the frame at the bottom.

Thread the H-harness D-ring attaching straps through the intermediate friction adapters, forming a quick-release with the running ends pointing away from the parachutist.

The H-harness was worn so that on the inside of the frame, the long straps formed an X under the intermediate bar. The friction adapters were positioned near the base of the frame and the straps were tightened around the rucksack. The snap hook straps were attached to the other pair of friction adapters all of which were part of a quick release system.

When necessary, further nylon straps with friction adapters were added to secure the load, either horizontally or to extend the H-harness straps.

In addition to the H-harness, an 18-foot lowering line was used, that could be taken from other equipment container models. This line was fastened to the H-harness straps at the X, folded in an orderly manner and secured with elastic

bands to the interior of the frame, leaving the end with the quick adjustable buckle free.

Having set up the rucksack, the H-harness snap hooks were attached to the parachute D-rings and the rucksack frame tied to the trooper's right leg with cotton webbing in a quick-release knot.

The lowering line was then attached to the parachute harness, passing through the right main strap and the right rear back strap loop.

After exiting the aircraft, the paratrooper released the tape keeping the rucksack frame to his leg, and at 200 feet, if there was no other parachute below, released the straps snap-hooked to the H-harness to drop the load, which remained hanging from the lowering line until landing.

Run the straps through the loops of the lowering line, insuring that the lowering line loops are aligned at the intersection of the straps.

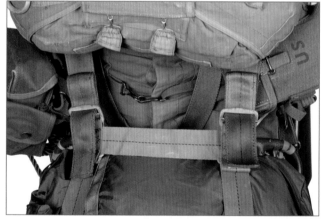

Pull the quick-releases of the D-ring attaching straps simultaneously and allow the rucksack to drop the length of the lowering line. The D-ring attaching straps should be removed from the parachute harness and secured to the H-harness before the parachute is turned in.

Attach a tiedown to the frame of the rucksack and around the right leg of the jumper, insuring that the quick-release knot is easily accessible.

Attach the lowering line to the parachute harness by passing the running end of the strap under and around the right main lift web and through the right rear backstrap loop. Fasten the running end of the lowering line to the quick-adjustable buckle using a quick-release fold.

Most of the soldiers taking part in the combat jump during Operation Junction City were equipped only with a Tropical Rucksack, worn as per regulations.

A few yards from the ground, the parachutist releases his heavy equipment, which remains attached to the jumper by the lowering strap, to avoid the risk of injury on landing.

Personnel Equipment Containers

When paratroopers carried extra loads in excess of their personal equipment, such as radios, ammunition or heavy gun parts, large multiple purpose containers were used.

If the additional equipment weighed less than 35 pounds, the jumpmaster decided whether or not to use a lowering strap, on which to suspend the container from the paratrooper's harness. In excess of

35 pounds, the use of a lowering strap was mandatory.

Adjustable Individual Weapons Case M1950

This was designed for soldiers to carry individual or collective weapons and consisted in a rectangular bag in heavy-duty felt-lined cotton canvas with a leather outer layer at the base to protect the con-

tents. It had a lateral slide fastener and a metal snap fastener. The idea was that the soldier, after landing, should be able to extract his weapon from the bag rapidly.

The bag was 10 inches wide, and adjustable in length from a minimum of 33 inches to a maximum of 50 ½ inches.

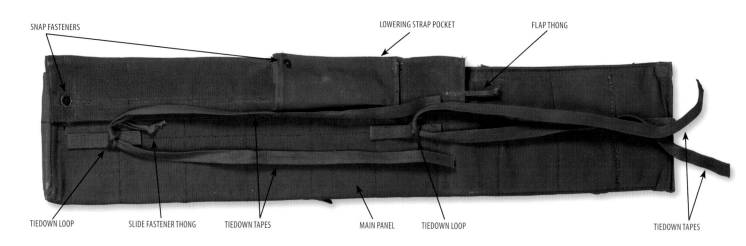

SNAP FASTENERS   LOWERING STRAP POCKET   FLAP THONG

TIEDOWN LOOP   SLIDE FASTENER THONG   TIEDOWN TAPES   MAIN PANEL   TIEDOWN LOOP   TIEDOWN TAPES

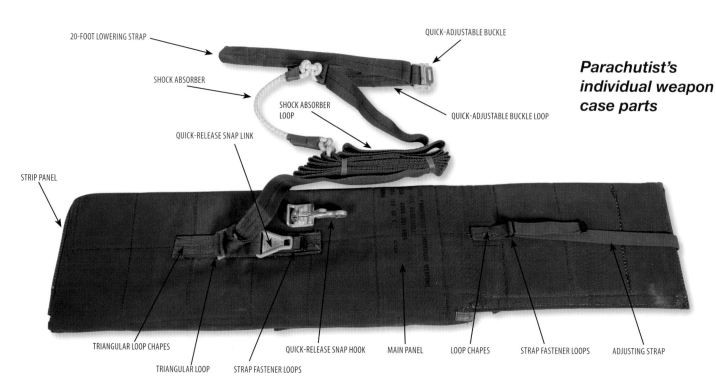

20-FOOT LOWERING STRAP   QUICK-ADJUSTABLE BUCKLE

SHOCK ABSORBER

SHOCK ABSORBER LOOP

QUICK-RELEASE SNAP LINK

QUICK-ADJUSTABLE BUCKLE LOOP

STRIP PANEL

Parachutist's individual weapon case parts

TRIANGULAR LOOP CHAPES   QUICK-RELEASE SNAP HOOK   MAIN PANEL   LOOP CHAPES   STRAP FASTENER LOOPS   ADJUSTING STRAP

TRIANGULAR LOOP   STRAP FASTENER LOOPS

124

Weapons were inserted muzzle down and with the operating rod facing outward. Then, the lateral slide fastener was closed and the top of the bag was folded to the size of the weapon inside and secured with the adjusting strap. If ammo magazines were carried, they had to be stowed individually to prevent metal rubbing against metal.

The bag had a quick-release snap hook that fastened to the left D-ring on the parachute harness. This hook was fastened to the bag via a quick-release mechanism that allowed the soldier to easily drop the bag and its heavy load.

To secure the bag and prevent it from swinging when the parachute deployed, it had tiedown tapes, of which one was tied to the main strap on the harness and the other to the jumper's left leg.

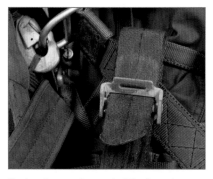

Fasten the running end of the lowering strap to the quick-adjustable buckle using a quick-release fold.

Another 20-foot lowering strap had an elastic portion to absorb the shock caused by dropping the suspended bag. At one end it attached to the weapon case by means of a loop, and at the other end to the parachute harness. This end passed between the left main lift web and the left rear back strap loop, and fastened to a quick-release buckle. The lowering strap was folded several times and secured with two retainer bands, and stowed in the external pocket on the weapon case for this purpose. When the lowering strap was required for use, the knots on the tiedown tapes were released and, at an altitude of some 200 feet, the trooper checked that no other parachutes are in the near vicinity of his path and freed the quick-release snap hook. This released the weapon case leaving it suspended from the lowering strap under the soldier, on the last stretch of his descent to landing.

Adjustable Equipment Bag

This item was box-like in shape, constructed of heavy-duty cotton canvas and measured 12 inches in width, 12 inches in depth and an adjustable length of 22 to 42 inches. Its purpose was to carry large loads, such as collective weapon parts, and the parts were stowed in three felt-lined compartments separated by pads to prevent damage from metal or wooden parts from chafing.

These bags weighed 13 pounds and could be loaded with a maximum weight of up to 95 pounds. It was closed with three securing straps and, on the ground, could be carried with its side handles.

QUICK-RELEASE SNAP AND
QUICK-RELEASE LINK

SNAP FASTENER

LOWERING STRAP POCKET

LOWERING STRAP

TACKING

HANDLE

SECURING STRAPS

HANDLE STRAP

QUICK-ADJUSTABLE
BUCKLE

QUICK-ADJUSTABLE
BUCKLE

RETAINING STRAP

SHOCK ABSORBER

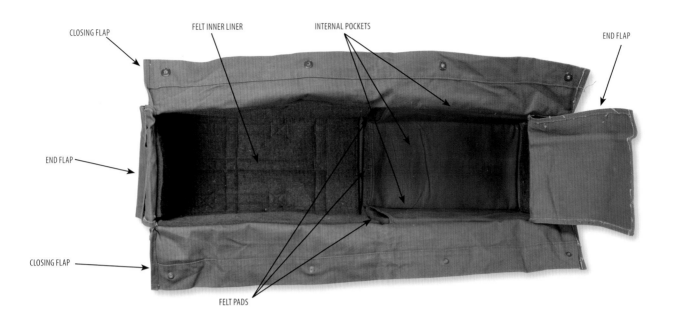

CLOSING FLAP   FELT INNER LINER   INTERNAL POCKETS   END FLAP

END FLAP

CLOSING FLAP

FELT PADS

To secure it to the parachute harness D-rings it had two quick-release snap hooks with a quick-release mechanism to remove it from the container.

To prevent the container from swinging, it had a retaining strap that was placed around the leg furthest from the side of the aircraft from which the jumper will exit.

The cord may be used on the handle of the quick-release snap to facilitate releasing the bag.

Lowering strap assembly.

The container also featured a lowering strap, similar to that on the M1950 weapon case, with a stretch of shock absorbing cord. The lowering strap was attached to the container by the handle on the top, and the other end of the strap was attached to the parachute harness, between the right main lift web and the right rear back strap loop. The slack in the lowering strap was folded and stowed in an exterior pocket on the container, as on the weapon case.

Detail of the shock absorbing cord.

After exiting the aircraft, the paratrooper followed the same procedure as with the weapon case. First, he released the retaining strap and at 200 feet he freed the quick-release snap hooks taking care not to collide with other jumpers. If the load was fragile, soldiers could be ordered not to release the container but to hold it on the quick-release snaps until after landing. It was also recommended not to release the container when landing among trees, as it provided protection against impact with branches. However, in the event of landing on power lines or on water, it had to be released completely and allowed to fall freely.

Weapons and Individual Equipment Container and Harness Assembly

This was a general-purpose system for carrying combat equipment consisting of a container and a harness assembly. The box-shaped container measured 12 inches wide, 12 inches deep and 36 in. in length, although it could be adjusted to 12 x 6 x 18 inches. The pack weighed 16 ½ pounds and could be loaded to a maximum total weight of 95 pounds.

Container and harness assembly.

The quick-release quick-fit connecting link attaches to the release assembly fastener.

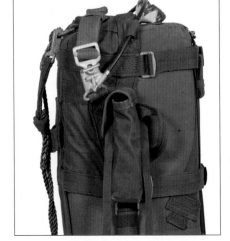

Detail of the cotton duck lowering line pocket.

Weapon and Individual Equipment Harness Assembly

The harness assembly consisted in a main cotton canvas body and a network of cotton-nylon securing and suspension straps, to which an 18-foot lowering line and a release assembly were added.

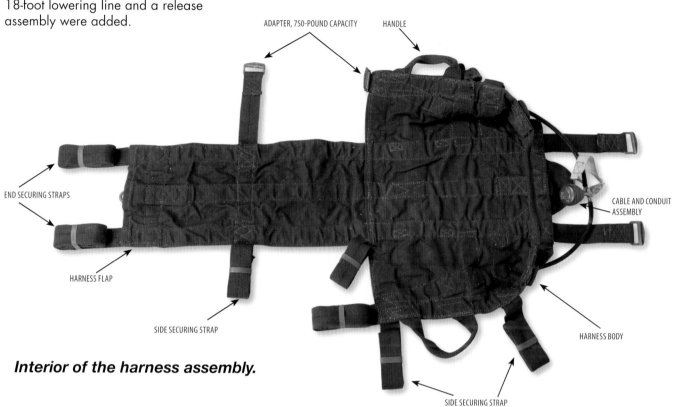

ADAPTER, 750-POUND CAPACITY · HANDLE · END SECURING STRAPS · HARNESS FLAP · SIDE SECURING STRAP · CABLE AND CONDUIT ASSEMBLY · HARNESS BODY · SIDE SECURING STRAP

Interior of the harness assembly.

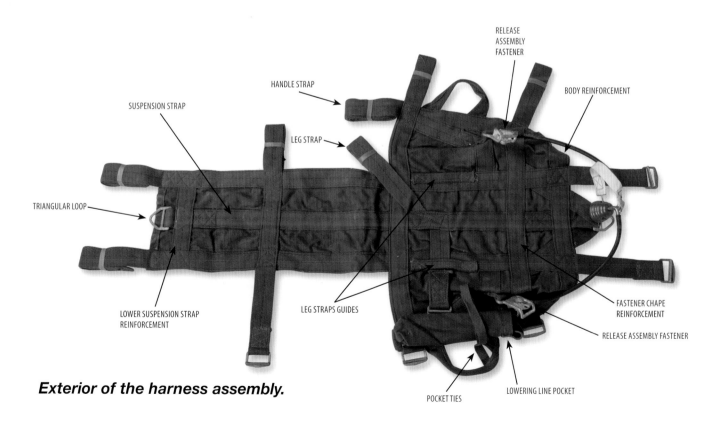

RELEASE ASSEMBLY FASTENER · HANDLE STRAP · BODY REINFORCEMENT · SUSPENSION STRAP · LEG STRAP · TRIANGULAR LOOP · LOWER SUSPENSION STRAP REINFORCEMENT · LEG STRAPS GUIDES · FASTENER CHAPE REINFORCEMENT · RELEASE ASSEMBLY FASTENER · POCKET TIES · LOWERING LINE POCKET

Exterior of the harness assembly.

The lowering line was a nylon cord with a snap hook on a nylon web strap at one end and at the other end, a quick-fit reversible adapter.

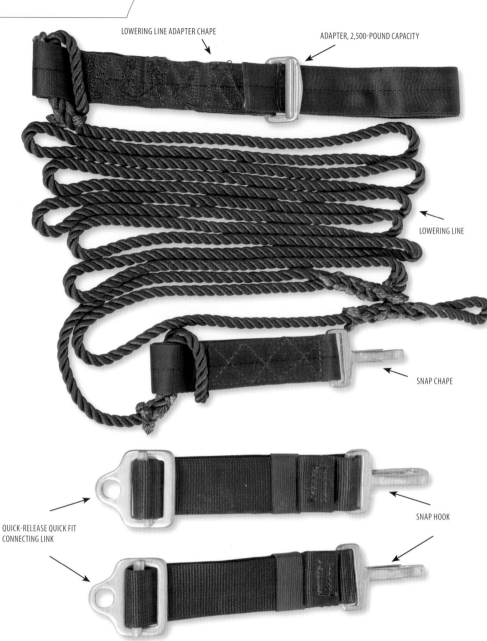

LOWERING LINE ADAPTER CHAPE

ADAPTER, 2,500-POUND CAPACITY

LOWERING LINE

SNAP CHAPE

Different manufacturers' marks.

QUICK-RELEASE QUICK FIT CONNECTING LINK

SNAP HOOK

The release assembly included a cable and conduit assembly and a release knob, as well as several straps, hooks and fasteners, in order to free the load rapidly and safely. To open the release knob the jumper had to pull the red ball up and out.

Each of the release assembly attaching straps or cotton-nylon webbing quick-release straps were equipped with a snaphook at one end and a quick-release quick-fit connecting link at the other end.

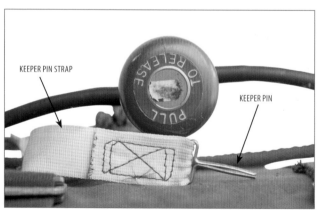

KEEPER PIN STRAP

KEEPER PIN

PULL TO RELEASE

Top view of container and harness assembly, showing release assembly parts.

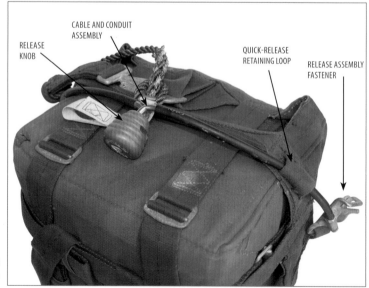

CABLE AND CONDUIT ASSEMBLY

RELEASE KNOB

QUICK-RELEASE RETAINING LOOP

RELEASE ASSEMBLY FASTENER

Weapon and Individual Equipment Container

When open, the container was a hexagon of heavy-duty cotton canvas, with a felt lining. Round the outside, it had several cotton-nylon carrying and securing straps, equipped with quick-fit reversible adapters.

Inside the container, items were placed in an orderly fashion with the softest, such as combat packs, at the point that will hit the ground in first place to serve as shock absorber for the rest of the load.

Having stowed the load and closed the bag, the harness assembly was attached, the container set on end, the straps were pulled tight and the release knob mechanism was armed.

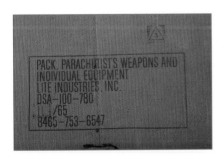

Different marks according to the manufacturer.

Deployment of the container. When the container body is fully extended, its maximum dimensions are 53 inches by 75 inches.

The lowering line was attached to a high position on the harness assembly, linked to a V-ring and to the carrying strap. The other end of the lowering line attached with the snap hook to the same V-ring if carried vertically, or to the V-ring on the other side for horizontal loads. Any slack in the line was folded and stowed in a pocket.

The Weapons and Individual Equipment Container was hooked to the D-ring on the parachute harness with the snap fasteners on the release assembly.

Additionally, it was secured to the trooper's leg with a leg strap fitted with a friction adapter and a quick-release fold.

The lowering line passed round the right main lift web and through the right rear back strap loop, and was fastened with a quick-release fold.

On exiting from the aircraft, paratroopers undid the leg strap, removed the cords keeping the lowering line folded and removed the safety pin from the release knob. At 200 feet above the ground they pulled the red toggle on the release knob and allowed the container to drop, suspended on the lowering line. In some cases, it was advised either not to release the container or to jettison it, following the same criteria for landing scenarios applicable to the Adjustable Equipment Bag.

Colonel Milloy, commander of the 501st Parachutist Infantry Regiment, directs operations during an exercise in the early sixties. Milloy fought at the Battle of Bastogne as a captain, in 1944, in command of C Company, 504th Parachutist Infantry Regiment. He served two tours in Vietnam, the second in 1969 as Major General in the 1st Infantry Division.

7. Insignias

The purpose of military insignias is to identify soldiers' status regarding aspects such as their branch of service, rank, skills, awards and unit. On dress and service uniforms, gold or silver plated metal emblems are used, or eye-catching cloth patches in brilliant colors. However, on work and field uniforms greater moderation is called for, with fewer emblems allowed and a preference for cloth versions. During the 1960s, cloth patches in bright colors were replaced with "subdued" versions almost exclusively in black. The regulations governing the use of insignias in the US Army, especially on work and service uniforms, changed several times during the Vietnam War period. Subdued versions of cloth patches were adopted to replace the colorful patches and, subsequently, metal versions were approved, likewise in subdued format, for insignias of rank, branch of service and skills. Moreover, in addition to changes in the materials they were made of, other changes were also implemented as to where the insignias should be worn on the uniform. In addition, in Vietnam, a more relaxed attitude was allowed toward regulations on insignias, partly due to difficulties with supply, but also to the widespread use of unauthorized insignias among the many different units to boost morale and esprit de corps.

7.1 Shoulder Sleeve Insignias

Shoulder Sleeve Insignias (SSI) are fabric insignias worn on the arm one inch from the shoulder seam, which is why they are also known as shoulder patches. The SSI on the left sleeve of a uniform represents the higher formation under whose operational control the soldier's unit belongs. Generally speaking, this is a division, although it can be another type of formation, either on a higher echelon, such as the case of "army", "command" o "field force"; or a lower echelon, such as a separate brigade. If worn on the right arm, it will show that the wearer has previously belonged to that unit in wartime, and is known as "former wartime service badge" or simply "combat badge". A soldier who is a veteran having served in several units in wartime can choose among his badges which to wear on his right arm.

In the US Army, all soldiers wear their corresponding SSI, except when wearing short-sleeved khaki shirts with the service uniform without coat, or in the case of dress blue uniforms.

Shoulder patches were made of cloth, with the motifs and background fully embroidered, resistant and of excellent quality. Up to 1966 they were made with cut edges, but from that year they were issued with the edges reinforced with an additional finish, known as mer rowed edge. Although in Vietnam the use of subdued patches was authorized as of 1966 for work and field uniforms, some units maintained their colored patches as a sign of pride and to reaffirm their tradition. This was most notable in the paratrooper units in Vietnam, such as the 101st Airborne Division that was deployed entirely to that country.

The first subdued versions of SSI were very simple, manufactured in Olive Drab Twill material with the motifs and border embroidered in black. These insignias are almost exclusive to the units operating in Vietnam at that time. They were fragile and deteriorated rapidly in the wash and exposure to sunlight. As of 1968 they were gradually replaced with versions similar to the colored patches, fully embroidered and much more resistant.

This Command Sergeant Major wears subdued insignias on his utility uniform, and subdued metal Master Parachutist wings on his utility cap. The Special Forces patch on his left arm shows he served in Vietnam with this unit. The man on the left is a veteran of the 187th Regimental Combat Team.

82nd Airborne Division

The 82nd Division was formed in 1917 and, with young men in its ranks from all 48 States in the Union, it was dubbed the "All American" while serving in France during the WWI. The badge contains the initials of that nickname, as well as the colors of the US flag. In 1942 it became the first airborne division in the US Army and added an "Airborne" tab to its SSI.

Cut edge patch with attached tab

Cut edge patch with separated tab

Merrowed edge patch

Subdued patch

101st Airborne Division

The 101st Division was established in 1923 in the State of Wisconsin, and its badge features the head of an American eagle in remembrance of "Old Abe", the mascot of the 8th Wisconsin Infantry Regiment during the Civil War. In 1942 it became an airborne division and the tab "Airborne" was added to its badge. In 1968, serving in Vietnam, it adapted to the new concept of airmobile warfare based on the use of helicopters, and was re-named the 101st Airborne Division (Airmobile).

Cut edge patch with attached tab

Merrowed edge patch   *Subdued patch*

173rd Airborne Brigade

S ince it was founded in 1917 as the 173rd Infantry Brigade it has been activated and reactivated several times. From 1963 it was established as the 173rd Airborne Brigade and the SSI with a winged dagger was approved, in allusion to its nature as an airborne unit, with the national colors: red, white and blue. It served in Vietnam until 1972 and was deactivated on its return to the United States, until being activated once again in 2000.

Cut edge patch   *Cut edge patch*

Merrowed edge patch   *Subdued patch*

7.2. Regimental Distinctive Unit Insignias

The U.S. Army Institute of Heraldry is responsible for the design and approval of military insignias in the Army. Each regiment has traditions that differentiate it from the rest, and these are reflected in the symbology on their devices. The distinctive unit insignia (DUI), also known as the distinctive insignia (DI) or unit crest, is a metal insignia derived from the coats of arms approved for battalions or larger units. These are worn over the shoulders on duty and service uniforms and are also displayed in combat leader tabs on work and field uniforms. These insignias were also worn as a pocket patch on field uniforms, especially in the 1950s and early 60s.

82nd Airborne Division
"All American Division"

101st Airborne Division
"Screaming Eagles"

173rd Airborne Brigade
"Sky Soldiers"

501st Parachute Infantry
Regiment "Geronimo"

 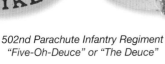 

502nd Parachute Infantry Regiment
"Five-Oh-Deuce" or "The Deuce"

508th Parachute Infantry Regiment
"Red Devils" or "Fury from the Sky"

503rd Parachute Infantry Regiment "The Rock"

Although the DUI were also worn on the front left of enlisted men's garrison caps, paratrooper units were an exception, since instead they wore the "Para and Glider Patch", common to all regiments. On field caps, the DUI was centered at the front but here, too, paratroopers were an exception to the rule as they wore their Parachutist's Wings, sometimes with the battalion oval.

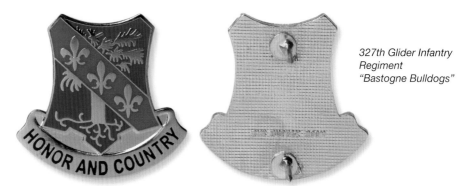

327th Glider Infantry Regiment "Bastogne Bulldogs"

7.3. Skills Badges and other parachutist's insignias

Throughout their military career, soldiers attend courses to acquire certain skills, such as parachuting, combat medical, explosive ordnance specialist, ranger, etc. Successfully completing a course leads to the pertinent diploma and the right to wear the corresponding badge. These insignias are usually metal for dress and service uniforms, and cloth for work and field uniforms.

Parachutist's Badge

Parachutist's Wings are awarded to Armed Forces personnel who pass the US Army Basic Airborne Course at the Airborne School in Fort Benning, Georgia. The design dates from the early nineteen-forties, when the first parachute units were founded in the US Army. In the sixties, young Americans were required to perform 24 months' active-duty service, or three years if they volunteered to select a specialty. Those aiming to become paratroopers, first of all, had to complete the Basic Training Course. Then they were sent to Infantry Advanced Individual Training, common for all soldiers destined for infantry, and finally joined the US Army Airborne School where the Basic Parachutist Badge was awarded after three weeks of physical training, instruction and five jumps.

In this photo taken in June 1964, two privates first class of the 82nd Airborne Division wear the cloth patch version of parachutist's wings on the work uniform (left) and the metal badge version on the duty uniform (right).

Metal Basic Parachutist Badge with pin back

Soldiers who kept up their parachutist activity achieved Senior Parachutist status after meeting a set of requirements that included 30 jumps and keeping their currency in an airborne unit for 24 months. After remaining for longer as a member of a parachute unit, the rank of Master Parachutist was attained after 65 jumps and 36 months' jump status.

Metal Basic Parachutist Badge with clutch back attachment

A further recognition, that stemmed from combat operations during WWII, was the Combat Jump Device, awarded to those taking part in a parachute assault on a combat zone. This status is indicated by a bronze star above the parachute wings for each jump or a gold star for five combat jumps.

Metal Senior Parachutist Badge

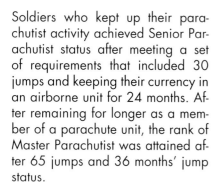

Presentation of the KREW Subdued Metal Senior Parachutist Badge in its packaging.

Master Parachutist Badge

Embroidered Parachutist Badges, color and subdued versions on OD twill

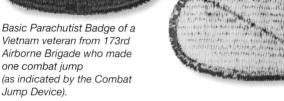

Basic Parachutist Badge of a Vietnam veteran from 173rd Airborne Brigade who made one combat jump (as indicated by the Combat Jump Device).

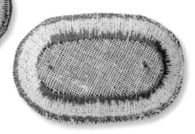

Basic Parachutist Badge of a veteran from HHC Battalion, 503th Parachute Infantry Regiment, 173rd Airborne Brigade

In the 1960s combat jump stars over parachutist's wings were worn for having taken part in airborne operations during WWII or the Korean War. In Vietnam, only a single combat jump by an American unit took place. It was in 1967, at the beginning of Operation Junction City, when a part of the 173rd Airborne Brigade was dropped, essentially the 2nd battalion, 503rd Airborne Infantry Regiment.

Subdued Metal Basic Parachutist Badge

Subdued Metal Senior Parachutist Badge

Subdued Metal Master Parachutist Badge

Presentation of the N.S. Meyer embroidered Parachutist Badge in its packaging.

Presentation of the VANGUARD Basic Parachutist Badge in its packaging.

143

Rigger Badge

The Parachute Rigger Badge was awarded to personnel specialized in folding parachutes. These "rigger wings" were won after successfully completing the Rigger Course, having previously passed the Basic Airborne Course.

These wings were worn on the chest over the right pocket, and on the front of the distinctive red baseball cap that, from the early 1960s, identified the rigger during preparations for a jump.

Silver Metal
Rigger Badge

Color Embroidered
Rigger Badge

Subdued Embroidered
Rigger Badge

Subdued Embroidered
Rigger Badge on OD twill

Pathfinder Badge

The Pathfinder course provided the necessary skills to take charge of controlling airborne operations in the field. Pathfinders precede other units on parachute drops, and their mission is to direct and facilitate operations from the ground. In Vietnam, the pathfinders controlled parachute drops of supplies and heliborne operations. The Pathfinder Badge is a winged torch that symbolizes their mission to lead the way for airborne operations. This badge, despite being worn unofficially since the forties, was officially approved in 1964 in patch form and in 1968 in its enameled metal version.

On field uniforms, the Pathfinder Badge was worn during the sixties centered on the left pocket, or on the front of the black baseball cap that identified pathfinders.

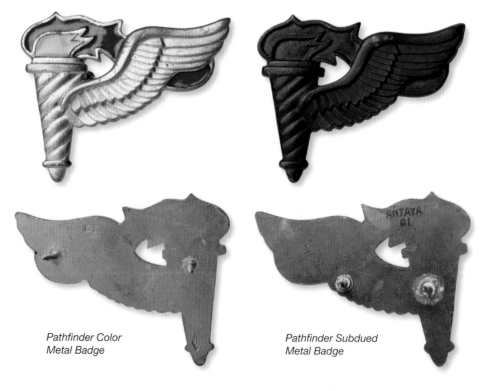

Pathfinder Color
Metal Badge

Pathfinder Subdued
Metal Badge

Ranger and Recon Badges

In the early 1950s, the US Army Ranger School was founded to train troops in small-unit operations. In the Vietnam War period officers were recommended to take the eight-week ranger course at Fort Benning, Georgia, so that, after graduation, they could promote the use of those tactics within their units. Graduates of this course we re entitled to wear an arched tab on the left shoulder, above the unit patch.

From 1958 the 101st Airborne Division encouraged officers and NCOs to take the ranger course, and graduates then trained others at the ranger tactics school set up within the division at Fort Campbell, Kentucky. Graduates of this school were given the title "Recondo", to avoid confusion with the ranger school, and were trained in small unit recce tactics.

The Recondo graduate patch was an arrowhead pointing to the ground.

Similarly to the 101st, the 82nd Airborne Division operated a Recondo School at Fort Bragg, where soldiers were qualified in a three-week course in ranger tactics.

82nd Airborne Division (Raider) Recondo School

101st Airborne Division Raider School

Parachutist's Badge Ovals

Ovals are used as a base to pin the metal Parachutist's Wings. The color represents the coat of arms of the wearer's regiment, and the battalion is indicated with bars across the colored oval. These have been in use since the 1940s and, although metal versions have existed, they are generally cloth patches with embroidered motifs. In certain periods of the Cold War they were worn on baseball caps, and even on field uniforms when metal wings were worn, but their most common use is on service uniforms, on the left breast.

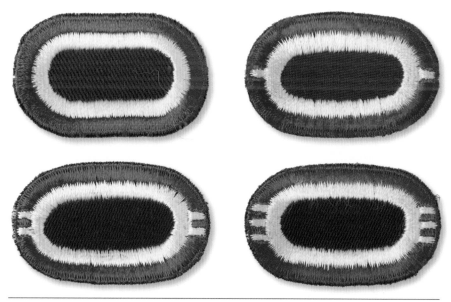

82nd Airborne Division

145

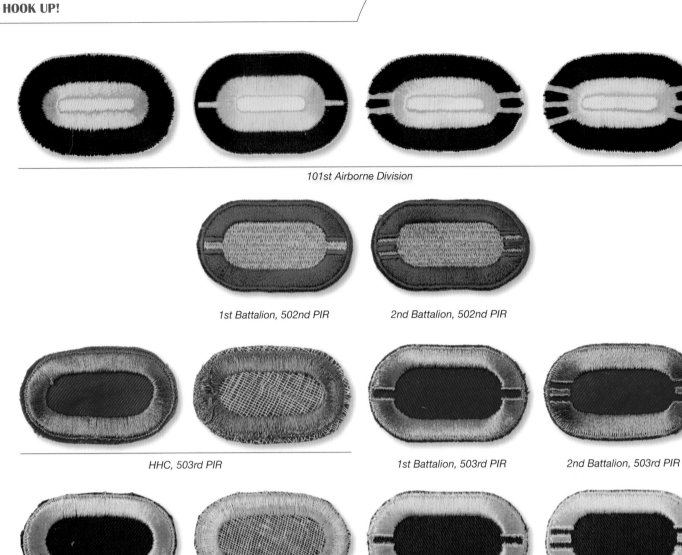

101st Airborne Division

1st Battalion, 502nd PIR

2nd Battalion, 502nd PIR

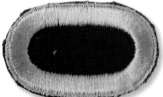

HHC, 503rd PIR

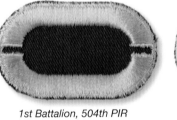

1st Battalion, 503rd PIR

2nd Battalion, 503rd PIR

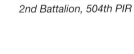

HHC, 504th PIR

1st Battalion, 504th PIR

2nd Battalion, 504th PIR

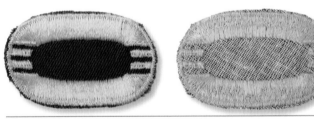

3rd Battalion, 504th PIR

HHC, 505th PIR

1st Battalion, 505th PIR

2nd Battalion, 505th PIR

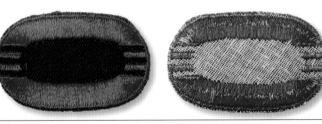

3rd Battalion, 505th PIR

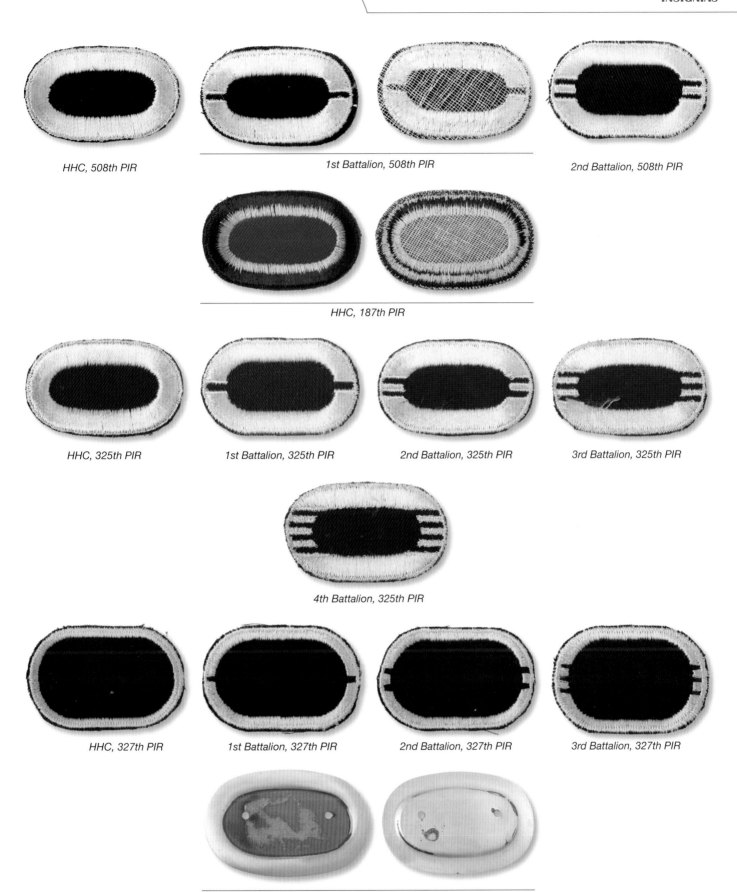

HHC, 508th PIR

1st Battalion, 508th PIR

2nd Battalion, 508th PIR

HHC, 187th PIR

HHC, 325th PIR

1st Battalion, 325th PIR

2nd Battalion, 325th PIR

3rd Battalion, 325th PIR

4th Battalion, 325th PIR

HHC, 327th PIR

1st Battalion, 327th PIR

2nd Battalion, 327th PIR

3rd Battalion, 327th PIR

Old metal model HHC, 503rd PIR. Some paratroopers preferred
the stamped metal ovals in the 1940s and 50s.

Paraglider Patch and Beret Flashes

During the WWII years, a device was designed for the new parachute and glider units, worn on the left of the garrison cap. The badge finally chosen was common to all airborne troops, with a central motif depicting a glider and a parachute. Enlisted personnel wore it on the left, while officers sewed it on the right and wore their metal rank insignia on the left. In both cases, the glider always points forward. This badge caused parachute troops to replace their DUI regimental badge—worn by other soldiers on their garrison caps— with the Paraglider Patch.

In the nineteen-sixties, the only US Army units authorised to wear a beret, both with service and work and field uniforms, were the Special Forces, after approval was granted by President Kennedy in 1961. During the Vietnam War, this garment was associated with elite status and its use was extended unofficially. After the war, in 1973, the maroon beret was permitted in parachute units, to become officially recognised in 1980.

The beret flash was used as a background for the regimental DUI worn on berets. The flash is made of cloth with the regimental colors embroidered, and, as in the case of ovals, the battalion was indicated by bars over the flash colors.

Enlisted Men Garrison Cap with Para-Glider patch

Warrant Officer Garrison Cap with Para-Glider patch

The glider patch always points forward

This private first class in Khaki Uniform wears his 82nd Airborne Division patch, and the oval under his para wings shows he belongs to the recce unit, 1st Squadron, 17th Cavalry Regiment. He is wearing the para-glider patch on his garrison cap.

82nd Airborne Division

101st Airborne Division

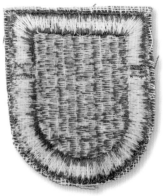

1st Battalion, 501st PIR *1st Battalion, 502nd PIR* *2nd Battalion, 502nd PIR*

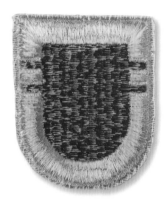

1st Battalion, 503rd PIR *2nd Battalion, 503rd PIR*

HHC, 504th PIR *1st Battalion, 504th PIR* *2nd Battalion, 504th PIR* *3rd Battalion, 504th PIR*

HHC, 505th PIR *1st Battalion, 505th PIR* *2nd Battalion, 505th PIR* *3rd Battalion, 505th PIR*

1st Battalion, 506th PIR

HHC, 508th PIR

1st Battalion, 508th PIR

2nd Battalion, 508th PIR

3rd Battalion, 187th PIR

Paratrooper of the 82nd airborne Division wearing the maroon beret flash and the distinctive insignia of his division.

HHC, 325th PIR

1st Battalion, 325th PIR

2nd Battalion, 325th PIR

3rd Battalion, 325th PIR

4th Battalion, 325th PIR

The Career of a
Great Editor
HENRY R. LUCE
1898 - 1967

**BATTLE
JUMP**

New tactics
step up the war

U.S. paratroopers
in mid-air
over Vietnam

MARCH 10 · 1967 · 35¢

*This issue of LIFE Magazine dedicated its cover and several pages to its article on the combat jump
performed by the 173rd Airborne Brigade during Operation Junction City.*

8. Manuals, Pamphlets and Paper Miscellanea

In the United States Armed Forces all procedures are regulated in the relevant manuals. In the case of the US Army, both the Department of Defense (DoD) and the Department of the Army (DA) provide a large number of publications aimed at soldier training and instruction, covering all situations, procedures, and use and maintenance of every type of equipment in service in the US Army. These manuals are kept updated and new editions replace and supersede the old ones. Generally speaking, this process is linked to the incorporation of new equipment as a result of advances in technology.

Another type of publications are those designed to care for troops' morale and welfare and *esprit de corps*. They include yearbooks, magazines and periodicals that are published by the airborne unit.

Publications that aimed to highlight paratroopers' qualities.

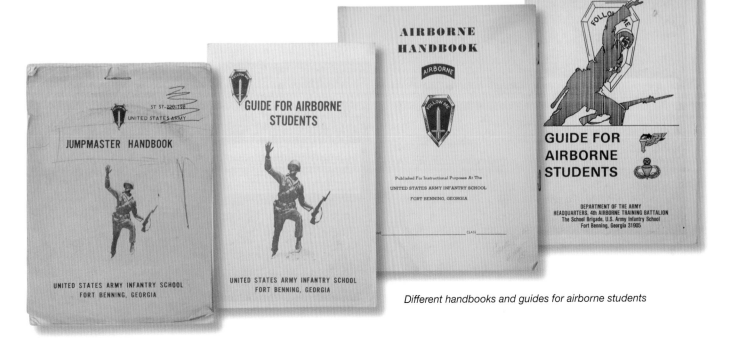

Different handbooks and guides for airborne students

8.1. Field and Technical Manuals

Some publications deal with general aspects of the different situations a soldier may encounter: examples of these are the Pamphlets (Pam) or the Pocket Guides (PG), circulated to all members. *The Soldier's Handbook* (DA Pam 21-13), for instance, was given to all recruits joining the barracks for their basic instruction period, and *A pocket guide to Vietnam* (DoD -21A or DA Pam 360-411) was issued on arrival in the country to all soldiers sent to Vietnam.

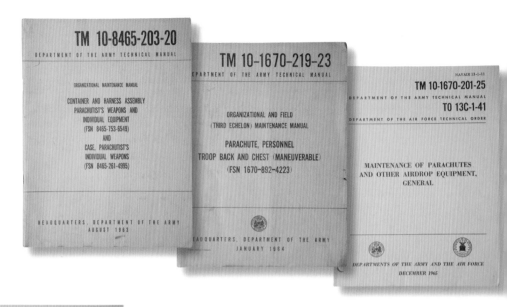

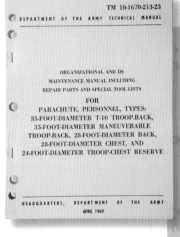
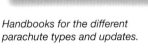

Handbooks for the different parachute types and updates.

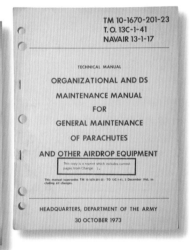

In addition to the DA Pamphlets (DA Pam), distributed on a general basis, the Field Manuals (FM) were fundamental military training texts, and the more specific Technical Manuals (TM) provided detailed information on concrete areas of expertise. All these publications were numbered with a code to identify the area, for example 9 was for Ordnance, 21 for Individual Soldier and 23 for Basic Weapons. Other less technical leaflets were also available, containing information of a more basic nature, such as the Training Circulars (TC), training or reference cards, or use and maintenance instructions issued with each soldier's equipment.

8.2. Parachutists Manuals

As when attending the Basic Combat Training Course and the Infantry Advanced Individual Training Course, students in the Basic Parachutist Course received a set of handbooks on the aspects that were specific to that stage in their training. The *Guide for Airborne Students* and the *Airborne Handbook* were published by the jump school at Fort Benning for stu-

dents in the elementary course, and provided information regarding the subjects taught during the course as well as barracks regulations.

Handbooks of a more technical nature were published either as TM or FM and were intended as reference books for certain processes and for equipment use and maintenance. FM 57-220 *Technical Training of*

Parachutists contained information on basic combat training, combat loads, jumpmaster duties and preparing for jumps from different airplane and helicopter types. Likewise, there were several Technical Manuals on different types of parachute, with a description of their components and their correct use and maintenance.

A group of parachutists awaits orders to jump in the 1950s. They all wear their equipment in the same manner and conduct themselves as stated in the procedures manuals.

Manuals such as this, "Technical Training of Parachutists", were superseded by new updated editions.

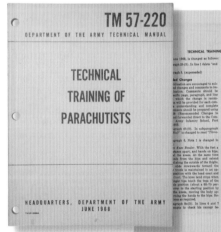

Until a new updated edition is released, changes were inserted in the form of supplements.

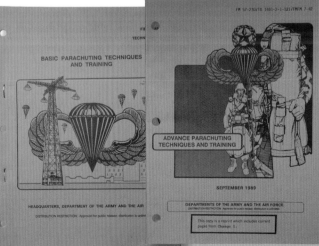

Several different manuals on parachuting techniques.

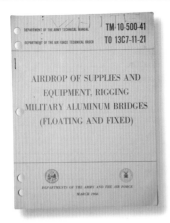

Special texts issued by the Supply Training Center of the Army School System

8.3. Parachutists´ paper miscellanea

During parachute courses, as in other military specialties, Airborne Class Yearbooks were published with participants' photographs and scenes from the activities they performed from the day they joined up to their graduation. In the 1960s and 70s the School Brigade had one Battalion Headquarters and nine Student Companies, numbered from the 41st to the 49th. Each Airborne Class included students from two different companies.

Every military unit usually had its own written means of communication, either in the form of a weekly paper or a quarterly magazine. In the case of airborne troops, there were examples such as the magazine *Rendez-vous with Destiny*, published by the 101st Airborne Division; *Sky Soldier*, by the 173rd Airborne Brigade; or the *Airborne Quarterly*, published by the Airborne Association.

Classbooks were issued to students after the conclusion of each class.

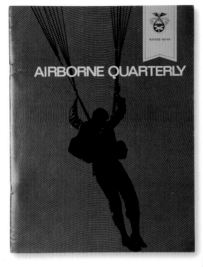

Magazines published specially for paratroopers.

The *Stars and Stripes* newspaper, dependent on the Department of Defense, covered the conflict in Vietnam alongside the world press, and through these publications troops were able to follow the reporting on their participation in Vietnam. Articles appearing in the prestigious magazines of the time, such as *Life*, covering the combat jump by the 173rd Airborne Brigade during Operation Junction City were highly appreciated.

The Vietnam War was covered extensively by the press.

BIBLIOGRAPHY

Anderson, C. J., **Grunts, US Infantry in Vietnam, Greenhill Books**, *London, 1998.*

Arques, Antonio, **Grunt, A pictorial report on the US Infantry's gear and life during the Vietnam war**, *Andrea Press, Madrid, 2014.*

Brayley, M. J., **American Web Equipment 1910-1967, Europa Militaria n°33**, *The Crowood Press, Wiltshire, 2006.*

Katcher, P. and Chappell, M., **Armies of the Vietnam War 1962-1975**, *Osprey Publishing Ltd., London, 1980.*

Leppeman, J., **Blood on the Risers. An Airborne Soldier's Thirty-five Months in Vietnam**, *Presidio Press, Ballantine Books, New York, 1991.*

Lyles, K., **Vietnam: US Uniforms in Colour Photographs, Europa Militaria Special n°3**, *Windrow and Greene, London, 1992.*

Lyles, K., **US Infantry Vietnam**, *Concord Publications Co., Hong Kong, 1996.*

Lyles, K., **US Airborne Vietnam**, *Concord Publications Co., Hong Kong, 1999.*

Mast G. and Halberstadt H., **To Be a Paratrooper**, *Zenith Press, Minesota, 2007.*

Mesko, J., **US Infantry-Vietnam**, *Squadron Signal Publications Inc., Texas, 1983.*

Monroe, C. A. and Pickrall, C., **American Web Equipment 1967-1991, Europa Militaria n°37**, *The Crowood Press, Wiltshire, 2012.*

Russell, L. E. and Chappell, M., **Armies of the Vietnam War (2)**, *Osprey Publishing Ltd., London, 1983.*

Rottman, G. L. and Lyles, K., **US Army Infantryman in Vietnam 1965-73**, *Osprey Publishing Ltd., New York, 2005.*

Rottman, G. L., **The US Army in the Vietnam War 1965-73**, *Osprey Publishing Ltd., New York, 2008.*

Rottman, G. L., **US Army Airborne EEUU 1940-1990**, *Reed International Books Ltd., London, 1990.*

Rottman, G. L., **Vietnam Airborne**, *Reed International Books Ltd., London, 1990.*

Stanton, S. L., **Vietnam Order of Battle**, *Galahad Books, New York, 1986.*

Stanton, S. L., **US Uniforms of the World War II**, *Stackpole Books, Mechanicsburg, 1991.*

Stanton, S. L., **US Uniforms of the Vietnam War**, *Stackpole Books, Harrisburg, 1989.*

Stanton, S. L., **US Uniforms of the Cold War 1948-1973**, *Stackpole Books, Mechanicsburg, 1994.*

Thompson, L., **Uniforms of the Indo-China and Vietnam Wars**, *Blandford Press, Dorset, 1984.*

Thompson, L., **US Airborne Forces of the Cold War**, *Greenhill Books, London, 2003.*

Richards, G., **World War II Troop Type Parachutes Allies - US, Britain, Russia**, *Schiffer Publishing Ltd., Pennsylvania, 2003.*

Wright R.K. Jr. and Greenwood J. T., **Airborne Forces at War**, *Naval Institute Press, Maryland, 2007.*

TM 57-220, technical training of parachutists, *Department of the army technical manual, 1952. C1, 20 July 1954. C29, November 1954.*

TM 57-220, technical training of parachutists, *Department of the army technical manual, 1956.*

C1, 11 February 1957. C2, 22 August 1957. C3, 27 March 1958.

TM 57-220, technical training of parachutists, *Department of the army technical manual, 1958. C1, 16 February 1960. C2, 16 November 1960. C3 C4, 16 January 1962.*

TM 57-220, technical training of parachutists, *Department of the army technical manual, 1962.*

TM 57-220, technical training of parachutists, *Department of the army technical bulletin, 1965. C1, 25 January 1966.*

TM 57-220, technical training of parachutists, *Department of the army technical manual, 1968.*

FM 57-220, basic parachuting techniques and training, *Department of the army and the air force, 1984.*

FM 57-220, basic parachuting techniques and training, *Department of the army and the air force, 1990.*

TC 57-1, the jumpmaster, *Department of the army, 1979.*

FM 57-230, advanced parachuting techniques and training, *Department of the army and the air force, 1989.*

FM 57-220, static line parachuting techniques and training, *Department of the army and the air force, 1996.*

TM 10-1670-201-23 organizational and DS maintenance manual for general maintenance of parachutes and other airdrop equipment, *1973.*

TM 10-1670-201-23 general maintenance of parachutes and other airdrop equipment.

TM 10-1670-201-25 maintenance of parachutes and other air drop equipment, general, *Dept. of army & air force, 1965.*

TM 10-1670-201-25 general maintenance of parachutes and other air drop equipment, *Dept. of army & air force, 1965.*

TM 10-1670-213-23 maintenance manual including repair parts & special tool lists for parachute personnel, types: 35 foot diameter T-10 troop - back.

TM 10-1670-271-23&p parachute, personnel type, 35 foot, T-10B, maintenance and repair parts, *1988.*

TM 10-1670-272-23&p parachute, personnel type, 35 foot, MC1-1B, maintenance and repair parts, *1988.*

TM 10-1670-292-23&p parachute, personnel type, 35 foot, MC1-1C maintenance and repair parts, *1988.*

TM 10-1670-293-23&p parachute, personnel type, 35 foot, T-10C, *1988.*

*of the 327th Inf, 101st Abn Div prepare to move across a rice field in search of
ong. (NARA archives).*

159